Get Ready To Live!

Book 1:

Living with

Purpose and Passion

Scott A. Rossell & Misti Rossell

Copyright © 2010 Scott A. Rossell and Misti Rossell

Printed in the United States of America.

ISBN: 978-0-615-35917-5

Library of Congress Control Number: 2010903616

www.GetReadyToLive.com

Disclaimer

By reading this disclaimer, you assume full responsibility for the use of the materials and information contained within the pages of this book. This book does not serve to provide medical, legal, or professional advice in any form. Under no circumstances will the authors or publisher be held responsible for any loss or damages caused by your use or reliance on the information published here or contained in resources related to this book including any associated websites, software, books, eBooks, documents, periodicals, audio, video, or other materials.

There are no guarantees that you will earn any money or achieve any specific results using the information in this material. Your level of success in achieving the potential results discussed in this book depends on your individual commitment, skills, knowledge, experience, and/or financial resources.

The authors have made the best effort to provide accurate information on the subjects discussed in light of the availability and accuracy of data prior to publishing. However, neither the author nor publisher assume any responsibility for errors or omissions that may have occurred and reserve the right to update the material subject matter as new research is made available.

Dedications

Scott

To my Dad who always asked "How?"
To my wife who always asks "When?"
And to all of my friends
who constantly ask "Why?!"

Misti

To Scott who never let me get away
with watching life float by.

Acknowledgements

Scott: No one reads this stuff, so why should I write about a bunch of people who helped us get this book in your hands? You don't know them. You'll probably never meet them. They're only important to me because they made this book possible.

Of course, I'm sure they would love to read about themselves here. Who wouldn't want to see their name mentioned in a book? And I guess it's only proper for me to mention the people who, without their help, we would be peddling this book on the streets or at swap meets.

So here goes...

To Robert Sanford, thanks for nagging the hell out me to finish this book. Your constant reminders that the subject matter has value, particularly during these troubling economic and emotional times, were always welcome and encouraging.

To Troy Beisigl, Angela and Robert Sanford, Brent Byerly and Catherine Weekly, thanks for attending our workshops in the very early days of development. Your insightful comments were priceless and your encouragement to continue without measure.

Misti: To all the best friends I've had throughout my life; Cynthia, Melissa, Janet, Kathy Jo, Leslie, Terah, Nancy, Deann and Vanessa for allowing me to be the kind of friend I love to be. A listener, a helper and one who has made you smile.

To Scott for his patience, dedication and love.

To Kim, Shan, Russell, Kent, Michael, Eric, Josh, Mom & Dad for your continued interest in me and my endeavors.

Contents

Introduction

1   rANdoM Decision Making   19

2   Your Specific Life Purpose   27

3   Your Greatest Passions and Dreams   45

4   The Passion Path System   53

5   Procrastination   83

6   Fear   99

7   Your Unique Abilities   111

8   Get Ready To Live!   121

    Recommended Reading   127

    Study Workbook*   135

    Ground Zero Page   151

* Additional free Study Workbooks are available for download at
   www.GetReadyToLive.com

Introduction

Congratulations on making a non-random human decision to start living your life to the fullest! (You'll know what I mean by "non-random" in the next chapter.)

I know that's a strange way to start a book, but it's true. You're going to find yourself reading phrases like this throughout the book and you might wonder, "Who writes like this?" But before we get to who we are, let's cut straight to the matter at hand. You picked up this book because you want to Get Ready To Live! You like the idea of living with Purpose and Passion. Right?! But what exactly do we mean by that?

To that, we offer you this promise, right at the start: Within the pages of this book, using a deceptively simple process, you will learn your specific, personal Life Purpose. And it's not a multiple choice answer. There is no quiz that points to one of a few cookie-cutter purposes in life for you to choose from. We don't attempt to pigeon-hole or label seven billion people in the world with just a handful of titles.

And it has nothing to do with politics, religion, "positive thinking", meditation, yoga, philosophy, metaphysics, drugs, vision quests, vitamins, martial arts, hypnotism, subliminal messages, exercise, astrology, numerology, palm reading, Zen, remote viewing, channeling, aroma therapy, public speaking, sales (of any kind), multi-level marketing, or networking.

But it does have everything to do with who you truly are. And only you can figure that out with the simple process we show you. By the time you finish reading chapter 2, you will have the clearest picture of who you are and what you were put on this Earth to do than you have ever had before. You'll know it through and through as the truest definition of who you are and your life will be forever changed for the better. And what's even better, you will have the strongest perception of your personal values and beliefs than ever before. This book doesn't change you, it reflects who you really are in perfect clarity. Once you finish reading this book and doing the exercises, you will be so much more of who you were before you started reading it.

The rest of the book is dedicated to showing how to make the best of your Life Purpose by examining your Greatest Passions and dreams and then giving you a step-by-step method to achieve them that really works.

We also show you how to overcome procrastination and fear and give you the tools to bolster your courage and make a difference in your life in whatever direction you choose. And finally, we'll show you that just as your Life Purpose is specific and one-of-a-kind, so are your Unique Abilities for achievement. We all have skills and talents. We also have fears and limitations. We show you how to put those together in a new, dynamic way that produces surprising and explosive results in your life.

So who are we anyway? And why should you believe us when we say we can show you something no one else has before? Please read on.

-=-=-=-=-=-=-=-=-

Scott: *My entire life I have suffered from a health condition that no doctor has ever been able to diagnose. It is similar in some ways to diabetes, hypoglycemia and narcolepsy rolled into one, but is in fact none of them. Consequently, it cannot be* *effectively treated and there is no known cure. I wake up every day in pain, too nauseated to eat and still exhausted in spite of a full night's sleep. I suffer from dizzy spells, joint pain, muscle pain, impaired eyesight and difficulty concentrating among a total of thirty-two persistent symptoms. The sun rips through my eyes and the slightest noises tear through my head. And at random times each day, my body inexplicably falls into a deep sleep for approximately four hours. Every day is a battle with my own body.*

As all humans do, I learned to adapt. I made the best of my more lucid moments which I called my "Power Hours". During these times when the pains were kept at bay with medication and the sleep was abated after a long unexpected nap, I would use every functional moment to find a solution for my condition. Doctors have so far proven less than hopeful. I quickly learned I'm on my own. I was forced to make unusual decisions in my life in order to maintain my career and my marriage. By drastically altering my diet, and insisting on absolutely no less than nine hours of sleep each night I was able to lessen the pain and nausea symptoms somewhat, but the random four hour bouts of sleep decreased to only two or three hours each day. I changed direction in my career in the information technology industry to become a contractor which allowed me a more flexible schedule. I even purchased a small RV with a full-sized bed and used it as my primary means of transportation so that I would always have a place to "crash" when my body insisted on going to sleep. It was a ridiculous way to live, but it was necessary.

During my "Power Hours" I pursued one of my Greatest Passions; reading. And not just reading, but researching. I thoroughly enjoy reading, highlighting important passages, taking notes and maintaining huge collections of related materials. My bookshelves, closets and garage are packed full of books, magazines, clippings of all sorts, journals and tons of notes. Having little time to enjoy my passion for reading, I learned how to read several books at a time, and very quickly. Most of the time, the subjects of my study were a search for solutions; a solution to my health condition, a way to organize my time more effectively, ways to avoid procrastination, and methods to help me concentrate and focus using whatever inherent assets I might have to overcome my challenges. I had to find a better way to live. I needed something empowering to help me overcome this ridiculous lifestyle.

I had tried everything legal, prescription or otherwise, to stay awake. Nothing worked. So I *resolved myself to learning how to make the best of my time and effort in spite of my condition. For the first time in my life I also decided to find the ideal career to fit my personality and talents. I read all of the books I could find on "Doing the work you love" and found some solace but not a complete answer. I studied the ancient writings of Epictetus to learn "The Art of Living". Helpful, but still no solid direction. I read every book ever written on "positive thinking" and that led me nowhere. In fact, from all of the literally hundreds of books I studied on subjects ranging from skills assessment to personality type to life simplification, organization, planning, numerology, anti-procrastination, herbal remedies, diet, physical fitness, religion, philosophy, and biographies of similarly challenged people in history, I never found one book that gave me the complete answer I needed. However, I took notes from everything I ever read.*

I learned that we all have a unique Life Purpose and that it is imperative to know what our Greatest Passions are in life so that we may live our lives to their fullest potential. I hadn't even considered it possible to know these things before. I just always assumed that we do the best we can to get from day to day with a basic understanding of what we like and what we don't like. It hadn't even occurred to me that I could have an Ultimate Dream. I was always too busy just trying to get to the next moment in my life. I learned how to eliminate fears and distractions in my life to avoid procrastination. And I even discovered how to use my debilitating health condition as an asset by determining my Unique Abilities!

Then one day, it all came together in a flash of inspiration. Like a domino effect, the pieces I had collected from varied sources in my studies suddenly fell together into a perfect design; each piece supporting the other to form an incredible system. I developed a method of organization for myself based on these concepts which allowed me to achieve amazing results in very short periods of time. What many would consider as just useful tools, I had to maintain as the only way to get through the day. By living my life in this manner, I was able to instantly jump into action as soon as my body would allow it.

I began to organize my life; eliminating distractions and clutter and optimizing the things that made my life work. It's amazing the huge effect little changes can have in your life when you simply employ a method to address them. I made a concerted effort to keep in touch with supportive friends. With newly organized and optimized expenses I was actually able to buy a condo and move out of my tiny apartment. I bought new clothes. I rearranged my office and was finally able to write - something I had been missing for a long time. I found the time, money and energy to travel - another of my Greatest Passions. I began taking vitamins and exercising. Me! Exercising! I noticed that the pain and nausea were more easily managed when I had more compelling reasons to wake up in the morning. And with my life in a more manageable condition I was actually able to think about other people's needs for a change.

The system I created to turn my life around is called The Passion Path System. It utilizes techniques that no other organizational or motivational system offers. And trust me, I've studied them all. By following this system on a daily basis, I successfully changed my life for the better. I knew who I was and how I wanted to live and I knew what I wanted to achieve. I overcame serious feelings of inadequacy and fear in my life. I approached issues using methods that were tailor-made for my specific Assets and Challenges which allowed me to accomplish amazing results in spite of my health condition. And I had a foolproof system that could not only help me discover and remind me of what was truly important to achieve, but also helped me maintain motivation and keep me on track, regardless of what life managed to throw my way. I had finally found the solution I had been seeking all my life! I was finally living my life to its fullest potential!

Even then, I had no idea just how powerful a tool I had developed. From my perspective, the methods I had adopted to merely get through each day of my life were simply crutches. But when I shared my ideas with others, I would watch them achieve amazing results practically overnight! I quickly realized that my "crutches" were like rockets to people who weren't held back by their body as I was. I soon realized that if a healthy person were to intentionally use the entire collection of techniques I had put together, they would be absolutely unstoppable!

This became even more apparent when my wife got involved. Each year we accomplished more and more. When we first started in 2004, my wife and I accomplished 16 major goals. It was an amazing feeling to achieve so much for the first time in our lives. In 2005, we accomplished 29 goals. In 2006, it was 36. By October of 2007, we had already achieved no less than 296! I remember because it was our anniversary. Two of the goals that year we achieved in one morning! By 2008, our goals had become more challenging and numerous, so we began to implement the system using software. My technical background and nerdly fascination with all things geeky made it inevitable. And that's when things really started ramping up. We started accomplishing major goals before finishing breakfast sometimes!

With a little encouragement from my family and friends, I considered sharing this powerful system with the world. My first challenge was to put it all together in a format that made sense. Many of the techniques required a bit of explanation. And that's how this book came to be.

This book will show you immutable truths about yourself that you would never have imagined. Not only will it show you how to recognize who you truly are but also where you are in your life and why. And it does so by showing you where to look within yourself to find the answers. The material in this book is supported by scientific research that proves there is a Science of Life that mathematically predicts with 100% accuracy your chances of success or failure in any endeavor. We then show you how to be 100% successful by using the laws of this Science to your advantage in your daily life.

*The material in this book has made my life a
wonder and a joy. It can affect your life even more
so. I hope you will decide to invest in the quality of
your life and commit to reading this entire book
and performing the exercises in each chapter.
They're fun and easy and will forever enhance your
perception of the world and your power to achieve
anything you want in life.*

*If there was a technology that could make a blind
man see and a lame man walk, how much more
powerful would that technology be in the hands of
a person without those limitations? They would be
superheroes. That's what this book gives you –
Superhero Powers!*

-=-=-=-=-=-=-=-=-=-

Misti: *I have always found a need to help others
deal with the problems life seems to hand out to all
of us. When I was in 3rd grade a girl named
Cynthia moved into our small town of Safford,
Arizona. Unlike the rest of us, she was very tall and
somewhat homely looking with a larger than
average nose. Her family was not very well off,
which resulted in her wearing the same homemade
yellow dress to school nearly every day. Soon the
cruelty of childhood presented itself and she quickly
became known as "Big Bird". The hurt in her eyes*

after a day of teasing was so apparent to me that it touched my very soul. I could nearly hear the voice inside of her head screaming at the top of her lungs from the agony and sadness she was feeling as a result of the constant pressure from the other children. I could feel her pain.

As much as I longed for the approval of my peers, I could not stand by and do nothing. I made it a point to be sure Cynthia knew that she had a friend in me and that I would be there for her if and when she needed me. Over the next year I watched as the effects of my friendship and compassion brought out the acceptance, smiles and laughter in Cynthia that every child is entitled to. It wasn't long before the teasing subsided and others found the fun and friendly girl I had discovered in Cynthia. The happiness that now filled her eyes was also in mine. I could feel her joy.

This is one of many memories that have come to surface after learning the concepts discussed in this book.

From the moment I met my husband he seemed to be on a never ending quest of self-improvement and self enlightenment. Book after book would pass through his hands, all of which resulted in deep discussions with me about what he was learning. Partly out of the want for self-improvement, but mostly out of courtesy I would listen to him and hear what he had learned taking what I thought I needed and dismissing the rest.

Three years ago he came to me with a new concept he had devised from the years of reading and research, which would assist in the recognition of our true self and living life to its fullest. I listened with the same courtesy I had always shown and half heartedly went through the step-by-step process he had created. At the conclusion, I did in fact come up with a definition of my true self, and assumed I was already living life accordingly. I had a job I loved. I was married to the man I adore. I had friends who valued me. Life was good. Life was comfortable. I didn't need more.

As life moved forward and as challenges and struggles presented themselves to me I soon found that I was not as comfortable as I thought. Things at work started to turn sour. Trusted friends proved unreliable and abusive. Life became one disappointment after another and I soon found myself wondering what I really wanted and what I really needed to be truly happy.

Seeing how frustrated and unhappy I had become, my husband again approached me with his concept

*of living life in accordance with our true selves.
This time I embraced the information and although
I came up with the same result as I had a few years
earlier, the meaning had much more of an impact
on me and I soon realized that I had not been living
up to my true potential. It's as if I always knew
who I was and how to be truly happy, but somehow
forgot or ignored the knowledge burying myself in
the challenges and expectations of life.*

*I was reminded that I am a compassionate person
who seeks out those in need of someone to listen to
them...someone to care and help if need be. With
this knowledge I have been able to identify what is
passionate to me and organize my life around
living and accomplishing what is important to me.
I no longer ride the uncontrollable wave that life
can be. I choose to live in accordance with who I
am. To do otherwise would be an injustice to
myself and to those I choose to have in my life.*

*An old college friend of mine once commented, "I
don't understand people who cheat at solitaire.
They're just cheating on themselves." Such is life.
I'm just playing a game of solitaire and I don't need
to cheat to win. I just need to know how to play
the game. Living contrary to who I am is cheating
and may result in a winning hand, but the thrill of
winning is lost. With the knowledge I have gained*

from the concepts you too will learn in this book, I
have found life fulfillment. I achieve more. I focus
on my passions. I dream. I live!

-=-=-=-=-=-=-=-=-=-

The lessons you are about to learn in this book are the culmination of my life's work. Like everyone else, I was looking for my way in life. And I am blessed with a Life Purpose that drives me to find solutions. So it should come as no surprise that I actually found the solutions I was looking for.

Just as someone who is lost in a jungle climbs a tree to see where they are and reaches the top of the tree to look out at the horizon in the distance, I have explored and found a clearer path to a better life that conveniently works for everyone.

I am no more intelligent than you are. I just have a Life Purpose that insists I explore to find solutions. I am simply behaving as I was designed to do. Just as you are right now, even if you don't realize it!

The writing is on the wall. I'm just here to flip the light switch on so you can see it. And I didn't write what's on the wall...You did! And when you read it, you will know without a doubt that it's exactly who you are and who you have always been. The writing on the wall is your Life Purpose and it never changes. And when you recognize it, you will experience the same amazing sensation we did that gives us unquestioned direction in our lives and unstoppable power in everything we do.

I know without a doubt that this book will change your life. And I look forward to hearing from you about your progress in the very near future.

At the end of the book, starting on page 135, you'll find a Study Workbook with all of the study materials you will need in order to complete the exercises in each chapter. I'll warn you ahead of time, when you finish reading this book, you will have discovered the most amazing insights about yourself and written them on the last couple of pages of this book. When we're done, I'm going to ask you to rip those pages out of the book and keep them on you at all times as a constant reminder of your discoveries. These Pages include the Ground Zero Page and a handy couple of Reference Pages. The Ground Zero Page is where you will write all of your specific discoveries about your Life Purpose, Greatest Passions, Dreams and your Unique Abilities which the Study Workbook will help you figure out. This will be the page with all the answers – all of YOUR specific answers. We'll be referring to this page throughout the entire book.

We call this page "Ground Zero" because the information you write on it is the one thing that is missing from all other self-help methods; YOU. Get Ready To Live! is all about who YOU are and what YOU need. And when life becomes too distracting, it helps to have a reminder that can bring you back to Ground Zero; to remind you of what's truly important to YOU.

The Reference Pages have everything you read in this book condensed into a couple of pages so you can easily carry them around with you to help remind you of the lessons you learned.

So, are you excited? We sure are. You've never read a book like this before, I guarantee it! And you're going to be blown away!

So let's get started. Let's...

Get Ready To Live!

Just keep movin'
straight ahead.
Every now and
then you find
yourself in a
different place.

- George Carlin

One of a kind stand-up comedian, social critic, actor, and author.

Chapter *1*

rANdoM Decision Making

In the introduction, we made some very big promises; Unique Life Purpose, daily Passion, and achievement of your Ultimate Dreams. These are no small claims. But, before we can show you how to achieve these things, we have to show you **WHY** you don't already have them in your life. And while we're at it, we'll show you why all other self-help methods rarely work in the long run.

In the self-help world, we hear a lot about "positive thinking". And while thinking positively and optimistically is always a good perspective to have in life, blind optimism as some would promote is just plain foolish. Positive thinking has even been packaged as a "secret" passed down through generations. Sadly, it's not true. It's a beautifully wrapped package of old ideas with a stellar soundtrack and impressive visual effects. This same effect is commonly referred to as "smoke and mirrors". It's a trick.

Fear management is another approach we see a lot of, which in a way is somewhat related to positive thinking and consequently suffers from the same failings. We may learn to overcome our fears, but that's simply eliminating the things that might hold us back while neglecting to provide foundational direction in our lives to take us to the next step. Still others use techniques to affect a physical "transformation" by bolstering confidence with carnival tricks like running across hot coals, which gives you a great adrenaline rush and pumps your system full of happy endorphins, but by the next day, you still have no idea what to actually do with your life.

All of these approaches are valid in their own right, if not taken too seriously as an ultimate solution. But they all lack the one key element that promotes lasting change and constant motivated progress. That element is Life Purpose; the only "transformation" that truly has a permanent effect; the recognition of your personal and unique Life Purpose.

But before we can discuss Life Purpose, it will help you to know how you got where you are today. Because no matter how much planning and goal setting you may have done in the past, I'm sorry to say, any successes you may have experienced up until now were due to blind random luck. And I can prove it with Science!

The true nature of random events can most easily be demonstrated with a game called Chaos. The Chaos Game was invented by physicists to understand the nature of random atomic events. What they learned is that random is not as random as we originally thought. But the nature of all random events are equally random. So, the haphazard manner in which atoms collide is just as random, as in our case, the hit-or-miss decision making we all attempt every day.

In any given situation, when we have to make a decision, we have three choices; Action, Inaction and Indecision. A decision for Action is a conscious choice to do something. A decision of Inaction is an intentional decision to NOT do something. And Indecision is a choice to do neither. And while Indecision leads to Inaction, it is not a conscious decision to not act. It is a choice to allow time or circumstances to make the decision for us.

The Chaos game shows us how these three random choices eventually build a pattern for our lives. The game is comprised of a simple triangle with three corners, each representing the three choices of everyday decision making; Action, Inaction, and Indecision. The triangle represents your life as a collection of all of the decisions you make throughout your life. A random decision is indicated by drawing a line from anywhere outside of the triangle toward one of the three corners to represent one of the three decisions. But just as John Lennon once said, "Life is what happens to you while you're busy making other plans", to represent the average success of each decision you make in life, you stop halfway along the line to the decision point and make a new decision. Each decision is represented by a single dot drawn halfway along the line to a corner point of the triangle.

In physics, the idea is that an atom will, on average, collide with another atom before it reaches its target. The same is true of human decisions. Our choices are often interrupted before we reach our goals. The next random decision picks up where the last one left off. Just like an atomic collision, the path is altered into a new direction.

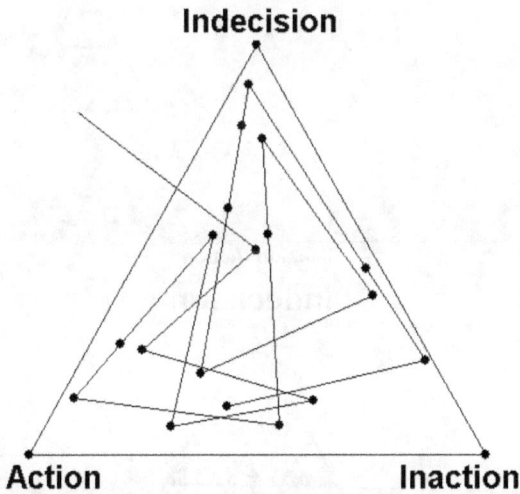

After thousands of decisions are made and charted in the Chaos triangle with a single dot for each choice, something really amazing begins to appear. This discovery was only just recently uncovered by scientists in 1994. By merely drawing random dots, a pattern emerges from these random choices. But not just any pattern. This pattern is 100% predictable and is a well known mathematical construct. This pattern is called the Sierpinski Triangle. And it was a complete surprise for scientists to see when the Chaos game was allowed to run through several thousand decisions.

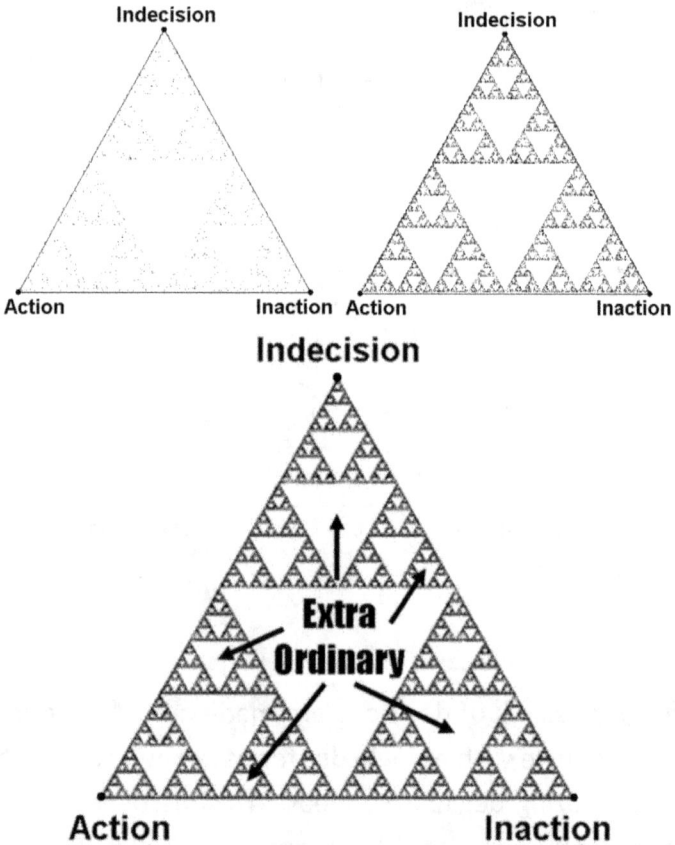

Indecision

Action   Inaction

Indecision

Action   Inaction

Indecision

Extra Ordinary

Action   Inaction

In this triangle, you see dark areas where random dots for each decision have congregated. These dark areas represent the common, ordinary results we all see every day from our random decision making. You will also see areas in the triangle that are completely empty. These are the places where extra-ordinary things occur. This is where we're interested in being because you absolutely cannot find your way into this extra-ordinary place by making random decisions! Even by accident!

When we talk about our ultimate dreams, we imagine great things; huge homes, fancy cars, successful careers, beautiful people in our lives and riches beyond description. Our big dreams are, by definition, extra-ordinary. And the only way to achieve your ultimate dreams is by making decisions that take you to non-random areas of your life. Extra-ordinary results require non-random decisions. The only way to achieve extra-ordinary results is by making specific, purpose-driven decisions on a regular basis. You have to learn how to stop making random decisions and start making purpose-driven decisions from now on. The good news is this is really easy to do once you know how and we'll show you exactly how in the next chapter.

People, for the sake of getting a living, forget to live.

- Margaret Fuller

19th century writer, journalist and women's rights activist

Chapter 2

Your Specific Life Purpose

Life Purpose is THE most important lesson in this book. But more than that, it is the most important lesson you will ever learn in life. Seriously. It's so important in fact that I must warn you about the changes that will unavoidably occur in your life the very second you learn your specific Life Purpose. If you're not ready at this time in your life to experience profound positive change, you may wish to tread lightly.

Once you learn your Life Purpose, it's a one way road that you can never back away from. It is quite literally like removing a dark hood from over your eyes. You'll notice changes in your perspective immediately. You'll see the world differently. And you'll begin to behave differently. And what's more, you're friends and family may not like it. After all, they're used to the way you were. And you won't be the same.

This reaction may best be illustrated by the natural behavior of the North American Blue Crab. These crabs can grow to be over three feet in size and have very powerful pinchers. This is important because when these crabs find themselves clustered together in a crab trap, they will complacently sit in the trap as long as the food used to lure them inside is still available. As soon as that food runs out and one of the crabs decides to leave, you would think they would all try to get out. Not so. When the first crab attempts to break free from the trap, the other crabs will attack it to prevent it from leaving. If that crab persists, the other crabs will actually tear it limb from limb to force it stay.

Our friends and family can react very similarly when they see changes in one of their own. They're not particularly evil or mean of course. It's a survival trait. We all try to conform in order to maintain a sense of safety in numbers. And it is this complacency in others you'll have to watch out for. People you love and trust will try to "help" you realize your mistake of seeing the world differently and acting accordingly. They need you to be the way you've always been. It makes them feel secure in their decisions and actions. After all, if you're suddenly looking at the world and seeing something they're not, it can be very disconcerting. So, when this occurs – and it will – be prepared to share this book with them so they can learn their own personal Life Purpose. Only then will they truly understand.

The good news is that it's all worth it. With your Life Purpose permanently entrenched at the forefront of your mind at all times, you will automatically make important, non-random decisions much more quickly and easily than ever before. And you will feel completely justified in every choice you make. You'll have a heightened awareness of yourself that breeds a level of self-esteem and confidence you have never known before.

A perfect example of this is when you're driving and you have a passenger who has never ridden in your car with you before. You know your car inside and out. You know how fast and how sharp you can make a turn. You know how quickly you can accelerate and how long it takes to stop. But your passenger doesn't. So when you turn into a parking spot or narrow garage entryway, you automatically turn the steering wheel and slip right into place without a worry. But they have no idea how close your front bumper is to the other cars or the wall. They feel uncomfortable while you're so into your element that you don't even realize there could be a concern. That is what knowing your Life Purpose is like. You will automatically, intuitively know your abilities and limitations while the people around you may become uncomfortable by the pace and determination you will display without hesitation.

So let's get started. The first thing you need to do in order to recognize your Life Purpose is to distinguish between the person the world thinks you are and the person you really are. The only way this process will work is if you can be brutally honest with yourself. No one else needs to know the answers you come up with while performing the exercises in this book. So being anything but completely frank with yourself will only hinder your success.

Something that holds people back at this point is an unwillingness to think about themselves selfishly. This exercise requires you to think only about you and nobody else. But this is not a selfish act. Rather, it is an exercise in self-ing. Self-ing is simply taking the time to honestly assess yourself; determining your true wants and needs, so that you can more effectively interact with society. It may feel a little odd at first focusing all of your attention on yourself, but it is vital you do so if only for the duration of this exercise so you can form an uncluttered and unbiased evaluation of your true Life Purpose. Others may have no trouble thinking about themselves at all and will easily move into the next step.

Once you've decided to properly focus only on yourself for the moment, you should then clear your mind of all preconceptions, judgments and assumptions about yourself. Forget about who you are in public; your roles in the office, at home, at church or just in the world in general. Forget about what you do for a living, your religious beliefs (just for a moment). Forget about your lifestyle and your sexual orientation. Clear all of that out of your mind.

Now, in the back of the book in the Study Workbook on page 136, under the heading "My Life Purpose", list all of your Positive Qualities. Are you joyful, charitable, courageous? Try to fill every line if you can. Make as long of a list as possible. Are you intelligent, strong, funny? Take as much time as you need. There is no time limit. Are you organized, honest, sociable? List every possible word that describes you in a positive manner.

Once you've exhausted your mind of all possible, truthful words that describe your Positive Qualities, you then need to narrow the list down to the one quality that best describes you. Sure, you may be funny and organized, but which one word best describes you more? Are you funny to the point that you know you could easily be a stand-up comedian? Or are you so organized that you could quickly sort out your entire garage and know where every little thing is located?
Some people are lucky enough to be able to look at their list of Positive Qualities and the one word that best describes them just pops off the page. Others may need a little help. If you fall into the second group, it may help if you approach the task systematically. Compare just the

first two words on the list. Of those two words, choose the one word that best describes you, cross the other one out and then compare the remaining word with the next word on the list. Continue down the list comparing only two words at a time and crossing out the word that describes you less until only one word remains. When you have narrowed the list down to one word, circle it. Congratulations! You're halfway there! The word you circled is the first word that describes your Life Purpose.

In the Study Workbook on page 151 is your Ground Zero Page. This is the most important section of the whole book. This is where you will write all of your specific discoveries about yourself. (This is one of the pages I'll ask you later to rip out and keep on you for future reference). For now, write the word you just circled on the first line under "**My Life Purpose: I am a(n)...**" on the Ground Zero Page. And while you're here, go ahead and write today's date on the first line next to "Life Path Anniversary Date:". Today is the first day of the rest of your life!

Now for the second part of your Life Purpose. Back on page 136, on the right side, list the Behaviors and Activities that you enjoy. It may be helpful to try to finish the sentence "My life works best or I am happiest when I am doing, being or having (something)." Do you enjoy reading, creating, or building? Or are you more of a listener who enjoys comforting others or just simply sitting and thinking? Here again, try to fill every line in the right side column. Do you enjoy camping, collecting, photographing? It doesn't have to make sense to anyone but yourself. Remember, for the time being, you're performing an exercise in self-ing. If you're happiest when you are debating, fighting, digging, or racing, write it down. If you feel satisfaction being strong, fast or beautiful, write it down. If you like simply having money, land, collectibles, baseball cards, whatever, write it down.

Here's a more extreme example. If you love to eat; I mean you truly enjoy food, write it down. Don't bother yourself with what others might think. Don't worry yourself with thoughts of social expectations about your appearance or weight. If you love the smell, taste and texture of food and love to eat it, then write it down. I cannot stress enough how important it is that you be completely honest with yourself. Remember, no one else need ever know what you wrote down here.

Once you've exhausted your mind of all the things you enjoy, you then need to sort and combine your list into groups on page 137. You'll notice the page is divided into six sections. Write the first word on your list of Behaviors and Activities from page 136 on the first line of the first section. Then continue on to the next word on your list. If the next word is similar to the previous word, write it down in the same section. If it is completely unrelated, then write it in the next section. Only you can decide if the words are similar or not. And whatever you group together is the right answer for you. If you feel photographing and organizing are similar because you like to keep very organized collections of your photos, then group them together. If you feel that being sociable and eating are similar, group them together.

Continue through your list of enjoyable Behaviors and Activities until you have sorted and grouped all of them into the sections on page 137. Try to group the words into five sections and use the sixth section as a catch-all for the words you're not quite sure where they go. Don't worry if you don't use all six sections. But try to find similarities between words to limit your use to just five.

Once you have completely sorted all of your Behaviors and Activities, read them over again, choose the one category that you most enjoy, and write #1 in the box on the bottom left of the section. Don't worry, we'll come back to the other categories a little later. We're not going to ignore them. We're just interested in the most important one right now.

Now this is very important! You need to find the EXACT word that describes this #1 category. It may already be on the list, but more likely you'll have to take the time to create a mental image of all of the words in the category to get a visual idea of what all of the words in the category represent. It might also help to use a dictionary or thesaurus to find the exact word. This can take a while.

Take the time. You only have to do this once in your life, but you want your answer to be as accurate as possible.

Once you determine the word that best describes your #1 category, it may help to adapt the word to fit the description of your Life Purpose better. For example, if your final word is "writing", it may help to adapt it to "writer" to fit the first word of your Life Purpose. In my case, my original words were "Curious" and "Exploring". I adapted the second word to "Explorer" so my Life Purpose ended up being "Curious Explorer".

Your Life Purpose should start with "I am a/an..." And once you determine the two words that describe your Life Purpose, this sentence is the most powerful phrase you will ever utter. It is like your own personal mantra; a secret formula made just for you. And it can never be taken away from you. Consequently, you also cannot get rid of it. It is who you are; who you have always been.

When you finally hit on the right word combination it should snap in your mind. You should begin to feel a special sensation growing in your mind that feels very, very right. Write that word down at the bottom of the category and circle it! Then, on your Ground Zero Page on page 151, write this word on the line next to the first word of your Life Purpose.

Almost immediately upon realizing your Life Purpose you'll begin to see profound positive changes in your perspective. You'll quickly learn what your Life Purpose means to you. With every choice and decision that comes your way, you now automatically compare it to your Life Purpose and you suddenly see where you have wasted so much time in the past. Decisions you previously made out of guilt or feelings of obligation or just plain random acceptance, now become less complicated.

STOP!

This is huge! (No, not the letters that spell "Stop".) You just discovered your specific Life Purpose! It is unique to you. There are seven billion people in the world and you now know your specific life purpose! Sit back and let that sink in a bit. You just re-discovered who you are. They don't hand this too you when you're born (wouldn't it be great if they did?!)

I envy the sensation you're feeling right now. I'm actually getting the chills as I type this because I remember how I felt when I discovered my Life Purpose. It was as if all of the planets aligned and every vibration and sound in the universe stopped to take notice of a spectacular event. My life flashed before my eyes and I saw a rapid montage of all the time I had wasted on random choices, false starts and bad decisions along with all the seemingly lucky breaks and good times and I knew - **I KNEW** each and every one of them for what they were; accidental random coincidences that were off the map of my Life Purpose when my life was not working for me and spot on when it was.

It was at that very moment that I realized I could now and forever choose the non-random paths that matched the very essence of my being. I felt charged and mind-bogglingly powerful. As if I were literally hovering over the controls for the direction of the rest of my life. As I sat and thought about the ramifications of this event, I began to realize the immensity of it all. I no longer had to justify my choices, my Life Purpose made it automatic for me. It didn't matter if no one else understood. There's nothing I could do about it anyway. I can't change who I am. And now that I know my Life Purpose, I can never forget it.

For example, there are many things I have yet to find interest in simply because I have never taken the time to explore them. But because I know myself and, more importantly, I know my Life Purpose as a Curious Explorer, when I'm asked to join someone to see or do something I've never done before, I'm much more inclined to explore. I choose to be involved not out of guilt or in an attempt to be sociable or amenable, but because I know without a doubt that I am a Curious Explorer and it's in my nature to explore; to see new things and experience new ideas. This is exactly what will happen with you and your Life Purpose. You'll automatically make non-random decisions that perfectly fit your Life Purpose. And you'll begin to notice more and more as each day passes, just how rooted your Life Purpose is within your daily life.

What's really amazing about individual Life Purpose is that the core purpose never changes; ever. But as you begin to live your life by your Life Purpose, instead of randomly as you did before, you begin to clarify your Life Purpose even more. This may eventually lead you to refine the definition of your Life Purpose because in living it you have realized more specific behaviors in yourself that you had never recognized before.

For example, in my own case, I knew my Life Purpose as a Curious Explorer for nearly a decade until in 2007 while hosting a workshop, I ran through the process for myself again and realized WHY I was a Curious Explorer. I realized that I explore for the sheer enjoyment of archiving my explorations. I live to read and research so I can take notes and write a book to share my discoveries. I travel so

I can photograph where I've been. I use a database to track my movie collection. I use a database to catalog my music collection. I spend hours researching and collecting information that ends up in one of several archival locations; a daily diary, a chronological photo collection, a computer file server. Always my explorations were for the purpose of archiving. And anyone who knows me knows that I never throw anything away.

So in 2007, I refined my Life Purpose from "Curious Explorer" to "Explorative Archivist". The original definition of my Life Purpose was no less true, it was just not near as accurate. Keep this in mind and consider using the method described in this chapter again in a couple of years to see if you have clarified your Life Purpose while living it. It never occurred to me to even try to rethink my Life Purpose for ten years because of the profound effect it had on my life. Imagine what a refined Life Purpose has done for me.

Knowing your Life Purpose is without a doubt the most liberating sensation you will ever experience. It automatically justifies your decisions in every conceivable circumstance; trivial or otherwise. And you quickly learn that it doesn't matter if anyone else understands. You know you're not being rash, callous or thoughtless when you make certain decisions based on your automatic understanding of your Life Purpose. But people around you may not understand your ability to make such swift decisions and choices.

So be prepared. Your Life Purpose is what it is. It always has been, even if you didn't recognize it acting in your life in the past. There's nothing you or anyone else can do to change that. And when you think back in your life when things were going well for you, it's highly likely that you were unknowingly living your life in accordance with your Life Purpose. Similarly, when your life was not going so well, you were probably living contrary to your Life Purpose. These are the realizations you will have. Your Life Purpose is who you have always been.

It's also very important for you to realize that true purpose in life comes from within. It's easy to accept outside motivations as purpose in life, because they are valid life purposes – just someone else's; religion, politics, tradition, social or geographical limits. And the people in your life who have accepted these purposes for their lives feel just as adamant and justified as you do in living your Life Purpose. The difference is you took the time to find your Unique Life Purpose.

In Shakespeare's Hamlet, Polonius tells his son "to thine own self be true." My take of that is "If you're not going to be yourself, who else are you going to be?" Think about that for a minute. Who's life had you been living before you discovered your own Life Purpose? Were you living by the traditions of your family? Were you living the hopes and dreams of your parents? Were you living the precepts of your religion simply because it is your religion? Is your career based on the fact that your parents were in the same field or you live in a geographic region that has limited options?

Now that you know your Life Purpose, it is impossible <u>not</u> to be honest with yourself. You will look at every aspect of your life and quickly realize that some things are completely and happily compatible. But you will also see some things that deep in your heart you always knew didn't quite fit who you are but you never before had a way to justify those feelings. Now, with your Life Purpose in mind, you will feel completely justified in altering those parts of your life that were never truly part of who you really are.

But it doesn't stop there. Life Purpose is only half of the key to living life to its fullest. The other half are your Greatest Passions; the activities that excite you to wake up every morning to get started on your day. And after you read the next chapter, you will be so energized and excited to get started in your new life that you may feel like a spinning top, bouncing from wall to wall wondering what to do first. Don't worry, we've been there too.

That's why we've included the following chapters to show you how to focus all of that energy in a way that really works. Just imagine how it will feel to know who you truly are, what you really want, and how to achieve it every waking hour of your life.

I have no special gift. I am only passionately curious.

- **Albert Einstein**

Theoretical physicist, philosopher and author

Chapter 3

Your Greatest Passions and Dreams

The other half of living your life to the fullest are your Greatest Passions; the activities that excite you to wake up and get started on your day. Just imagine waking up and actually hopping out of bed, excited to do the things that truly matter to you. After you perform the exercises in this chapter you will know exactly what you want to achieve in your life. And later in chapter 4 we'll show you exactly how to do it.

Your Greatest Passions are the enjoyable Behaviors and Activities you listed and sorted in the six sections on page 137 while discovering your Life Purpose; the section you marked with the number one. Remember when I said earlier we'd come back to this page? Let's go back there now. Re-read the remaining sections. In each of the remaining boxes, write the numbers two through six in the order in which each section is most import to you. The first one, which you already marked #1, is your Life Purpose and coincidentally, your #1 Greatest Passion. The second one, marked #2 is your #2 Greatest Passion and so on. Although there are six sections, we're only interested in your top five. Once you've completed scoring the other five sections, you might consider the words listed in the remaining "catch all" sixth section to see if they can be included in any of the other five. The desired end result is your top five Greatest Passions with the first one also being your Life Purpose with all of your Enjoyable Behaviors and Activities accounted for.

Beginning on page 138 of your Workbook, you'll find a separate page for each of your five Greatest Passions. For each one, write a short phrase on the top line that specifically describes WHY you enjoy that specific Passion. Why are these important to you? While you're thinking about this, remember the difference between self-ing and self-ish. Taking the time to think in a self-ing manner to know yourself and what you need and want helps you to interact with society much more effectively and less selfishly.

These positive phrases describe your Greatest Passions; the reason why you enjoy these activities. For example, I enjoy writing because it allows me to share the interesting things I have found.

Below each Passion, there is room to write three hyper-detailed milestones. Milestones are indicators that show you when you are living a passion to its fullest, just like mile markers show your progress from point A to point B on a map.

You must be very specific here. Detail is key in this exercise. Think of it as if you are dealing with a tricky genie who will give you exactly what you ask for. If you asked the genie for a Corvette, poof, he gives you a Corvette. Of course, being the tricky genie he is, since you weren't specific, the Corvette you get is not what you expected. It's not the right year, model or color and in fact it's a little toy that sits on your desk. Next wish!

Don't be vague or leave anything to chance when describing these milestones. The best way to write these milestones is to answer the questions: Who, What, When, Where, How and Why for each milestone. It helps to start with a clear image of where you ultimately want to be with that Passion in your life. Be as creative as possible. And write your milestones in the past tense as if you have already achieved them. That way, you know what your achievement should look like when it is done.

An example from my passions is Writing. I love to write. It is a powerful tool to express my thoughts while simultaneously requiring me to verify and refine them. You truly do not understand a subject fully until you try to teach it and that's what writing does for me. In my office, I have a note tacked to my bulletin board that says "Writing is the ultimate money for nothing career." And it's true, for me anyway. All I have to do is figure out how to press keys on a keyboard at whatever time of the day I choose in order to convey my thoughts. Each key press is free and the cumulative effort is an entire book. I find that amazing.

So, my first milestone is:

1. *"I have written and had several popular books published while living in Del Mar California by my 45th birthday which earn me a stable and more than adequate income so I may more freely travel and explore while investing for a very comfortable retirement while continuing my writing on my own schedule."*

Notice the details in this one milestone:

- **Who:** "I have written" - Not ghost written. I wrote my own books.

- **What:** "had several popular books published" – Not just one or two books and they were actually published. "popular" - Not books just sitting on a shelf and unknown, but actually popular. And "books" - Not articles.

- **When:** "by my 45th birthday" – I'd like to start travelling much more at that age.

- **Where:** "Del Mar California" – My home.

- **How:** "earn me" - Not just earning money for someone else. And "a stable and more than adequate income" - Not just a livable income.

- **Why:** "so I may more freely travel and explore while investing for a very comfortable retirement while continuing my writing on my own schedule." – Following my Life Purpose; exploration, travel, writing. And living a comfortable retirement writing when the muse strikes.

Without this level of detail in your milestones you will not be able to use the information in the next chapter to properly identify and prioritize your goals. And the tools we give you in the next chapter are the most powerful, long-standing, get-it-done system ever devised! But you have to give it the details to work with.

Now, go ahead and write three milestones for each of your Greatest Passions. I know this will take a lot of thought and time on your part, but it's really worth it, trust me. It can also be a lot of fun thinking and dreaming about how you will accomplish the most important aspects of your life.

Once you have written the milestones for all five of your Greatest Passions, turn to page 151 on your Ground Zero Page and write short summary descriptions for each as reminders. Following my example, my short summary for my passion would be "Writer". My first milestone summary reads, "Retired, published writer in Del mar at 45." Just enough to remind me of what I wrote in more detail in the Workbook. I can always refer to the Workbook later if I forget what I meant by the summary. In fact, it's not a bad idea to review your Workbook answers on a regular basis just to keep the details sharp in your mind.

Just as your Life Purpose may become more refined in the future, so may your Passions. Your dreams will certainly grow more ambitious as you achieve your goals. So you should repeat this process at least once a year.

At this point, you should congratulate yourself. It's only the third chapter and you already know your Life Purpose which gives you an automatic, non-random decision-making process focusing your efforts toward the attainment of your goals and dreams. And you know your Greatest Passions which guide your daily endeavors for a more exciting and rewarding life. You'll quickly learn that your Greatest Passions are the way you express your Life Purpose.

In the next chapter, you'll learn about the best system ever devised to realize your dreams: The Passion Path System. It has forever changed my life and I am confident it will do the same for you. I'm also very proud of the fact that it is completely indestructible and immune to the failings of any other system you may have used or read about in the past. This is where the rubber meets the road and you start to achieve your goals in ways you never expected and more quickly than you ever thought possible.

If today was perfect,

there would be no need for tomorrow.

\- Unknown

Chapter 4

The Passion Path System

I originally designed The Passion Path System for myself. I needed a method to keep track of EVERYTHING I needed and wanted to do without it getting too complicated or expensive. The system had to be quick to use, easy to handle and infinitely expandable. And it had to seamlessly include all of the things I had learned from my years of research on human nature, organization, task management, and motivation. So I decided to use nothing more than a stack of index cards and a marker. We do offer free downloads on our website of all of the materials used in this system, but all you really need is a simple stack of index cards and something to write with. I suggest a large felt tip marker to keep your cards short, to the point and easy to read.

The Passion Path System includes the Ground Zero Page and the index cards you will write, which we call Destiny Cards.

We've already worked with the Ground Zero Page in the first few chapters. This one page is the main method by which the entire system functions. It serve as a consistent single reminder of all the things that are important to you. And that reminder is key to keeping the system alive and functioning in your life. No other self-help method gives you this.

The Destiny Cards are the foundation of the system. Standard 3 x 5 index card stock is used to organize and prioritize your goals, habits, and dreams; basically, every aspect of your life.

This system is very empowering because it misses nothing while giving you only the most important things you need to do, one task at a time in the proper order. All other organizational systems eventually fail because of two simple oversights;

1) They try to impose external forces onto your goals instead of allowing you to make goals based on your individual Life Purpose.

This is hugely important! A popular matrix in the self-help industry suggests that all tasks should fall into one of four categories depending on the level of "importance" and "urgency" of the task. What this matrix fails to address however is that these are external forces which do not take into account who you are and what you truly need.

The Passion Path Destiny Cards are organized in a similar matrix of four categories but based on your specific Needs and Wants and the level of Importance that is congruous with your specific Life Purpose and Greatest Passions. In this way, you can automatically sort and eliminate tasks much more quickly and in harmony with YOUR priorities, not the "urgency" and "importance" of others.

2) They offer no method to stay on track in spite of outside influences or procrastination.

That's what the Ground Zero Page is for. They bring you back to Ground Zero to remind you of what's important to YOU.

While I'm not an advocate of New Year resolutions per se simply because they have a high failure rate, I do recommend that the process described below be performed at least once a year. Preferably every six months. I usually run through the process at the beginning of the year and again around July. My birthday is in July, so each date has significance for me as a good starting point for staying organized. Since The Passion Path System is a continual daily process, it can serve as a New Year resolution to begin and then continue throughout the year.

Most New Year resolutions fail because they are single, huge tasks with no details other than "lose weight", "get in shape", "finish my book", etc. These have nothing to do with your specific Life Purpose or Greatest Passions and are not shaped to match your specific Assets and Challenges (more about these in Chapter 7). They provide no details or milestones to help you know when you're progressing. The Passion Path System takes all of these into consideration and provides a consistent foundation for progress for the rest of your life; one task at a time, one day at a time.

While you're reading this chapter, you may at first become a little overwhelmed by the amount of sorting and prioritizing that is involved. Don't let this scare you. I assure you, it looks a little daunting at first, but once you take the time to understand it, it makes perfect sense and comes very automatic to you. There is also a video on our website that shows you how to perform this exercise step-by-step, so take a deep breath and dive right in. If you don't get it the first time around, don't worry, you will.

So let's get started. Grab a stack of 3 x 5 inch index cards and a large felt tip marker. Find a large flat surface to work on – the kitchen table comes to mind. Clear everything off the table – you're going to need a lot of room. We're going to be writing on cards and organizing them into several different piles on the table.

The first step is to get everything out of your head onto these cards; a brainstorming session to write down everything you need to do and everything you ever wanted to do or have in your life. Write only one item on each card and leave a little space at the top to add a line of information for sorting. We'll get to that later when we prioritize them.

While you're doing this exercise, remember the difference between self-ing and self-ish. Knowing yourself first is the best way to interact with society effectively and less selfishly.

Start out by visualizing every location and aspect of your life; work, home, your vehicles, friends, relatives, hobbies, repairs, purchases, vacation destinations, things you've always wanted to learn, habits to lose or gain, things to dispose of, relationships to maintain or eliminate. Everything from trivial tasks to dreams. And be brutally honest with yourself. Otherwise you're just cheating at solitaire. What's the point of that? If you feel you need to lose fifty pounds, write it down. If you have trouble maintaining the habit of taking the garbage out or other regular household chores, write them each on a card. No matter what it is; get a haircut, go to Disneyland, quit smoking, run for governor, write them each on a card.

Once you've taken the time to exhaust your mind and finished writing as many cards as you can imagine, you're ready to start sorting them. The first time you sort the Destiny Cards can be a little daunting, so take it slow.

You will be sorting all of your Destiny Cards into seven stacks

- Immediate
- Short Term
- Long Term
- Dreams
- Habits
- Trivial
- Purchases

To make it easier to remember each of the seven stacks, take seven index cards and write one of each of the above categories on a card. These will be your seven sorting header cards. Lay these header cards across the table in the order above. We'll be sorting all of the Destiny Cards you wrote earlier under these seven header cards. To make these header cards stand out from the Destiny Cards you wrote, you might consider using a highlighter to color the card or even use a different colored index card.

Go through the cards you wrote one at a time and determine if the card is an Immediate task, a Short Term goal, a Long Term goal, a Dream, a Habit, a Trivial task, or a Purchase. Place the card under the header card matching that category and continue until all of the cards are sorted.

Immediate tasks are things that need to be done right away while Short Term tasks can be done in less than one year, preferably within three months. Long Term tasks are either large projects that require constant small steps to eventually achieve (like organizing a movie or music collection ten titles each day), or tasks that cannot be taken care of until a later date or are dependent on other Short Term tasks before they can be attempted.

Purchases are tasks that require money to happen. Of course, just about all tasks require money to some degree, but these are tasks that you wish to set aside money specifically to achieve; a new laptop, a car, or a vacation. They don't have to be expensive items necessarily, just items that you don't want to forget to buy.

Once all of your cards have been sorted into their proper categories under the seven header cards, it's time to prioritize them.

All seven categories are sorted from most important to least. And only you can determine what is truly important and in what order. The most important card in each category, should represent the task you most need or want to achieve.

Purchases are sorted from least expensive to most so you can maximize your financial resources to accomplish more purchases sooner. You may be tempted to prioritize a higher priced item before less expensive ones because you believe you need or want it more than the others. Try to refrain from doing so. Each Purchase card represents a goal and the purpose of these Destiny Cards in the Passion Path System is to accomplish as many goals as possible. Also, the next step is a bit of an eye-opener.

Once you've sorted the cards in each category by priority and the Purchase cards by cost, go through each of the seven stacks again, maintaining the order of priority, and on each card, write in the top right corner the word "Need" or "Want" to indicate if the task is something you really need or just something you would like.

Now comes that eye-opener I mentioned. Keeping priority in mind, for each category of cards, move the Needs to the top of the stack, leaving the Wants at the bottom of the stack.

You should end up with all of the cards in each of the seven categories sorted with the Needs on the top by priority (most important to least) and the Wants on the bottom also sorted by priority.

The Purchases cards should now have the least expensive Needs at the top in order of cost from least to most expensive followed by the Wants sorted from least to most expensive.

Did you notice that some cards ended up lower in priority than you might have expected? That's the effect looking at your goals and tasks in the proper perspective can have. By using a priority matrix of four categories determined by Need and Want and what's important to YOU instead of outside urgency and imposed importance, you quickly see where YOUR priorities lie.

Keep an eye out for Booterfliez!

What are Booterfliez?

Booterfliez are simple tasks that can make a huge difference in your life but are incredibly simple to implement. For example, during a particularly rough patch in our life, we found ourselves constantly dreading opening the door to our home to find the answering machine waiting for us with nothing but bad news on it. So we got rid of it and the home phone along with it and relied strictly on our cell phones and voicemail. We no longer had to worry about what was waiting for us when we got home. We either got all of our bad news while we were out and about or when we decided to check our voicemail. I minor distinction, but it made all the difference in the world for us.

Another example was the installation of a garage door opener code pad. We had a detached garage. And had been using the remote to open the garage door. Sometimes, we forgot to bring the remote and had to walk all the way back upstairs to get it. So we installed a code pad on the garage so we could just enter a four digit code to enter the door and we left the remote in the car.

Simple things like this can make a huge difference in your life and make great Destiny Cards. They may appear Trivial at first, but after careful thought, you may find it beneficial to prioritize them a little higher because of the impact it can have on your life and emotional well being.

> *The word "Booterfliez" was given to us by Misti's brother Josh, who was studying to be an actor. It's a word used by actors to help them remember how to speak with a Russian accent. By saying this one word with a trilled "r", you have every sound necessary to approximate a decent Russian accent. Which has absolutely nothing to do with Life Purpose and getting things done in your life but it is an incredibly efficient and simple solution to achieve something as miraculous as changing your entire persona through your voice. So the word stuck with us when describing simple actions that can have a profound effect on our lives.*

Okay, back to sorting...Finally, one last time, go through each of the seven stacks, again maintaining the order of priority, and write the category name (Immediate, Short Term, Long Term, etc) and the current year on the top left corner of each card.

You're doing great! You should now have seven nicely sorted and prioritized stacks of Destiny Cards, each with a header card indicating each of the seven categories.

The first card in each of the seven categories should be the highest priority card for that category.

- **The Highest Immediate Card** – This card reminds you to eliminate those nagging tasks that you have allowed to have a deadline. Truth be told, no task is truly important enough to require your immediate attention until you say it does. The immediacy is not in the task, it's a judgment call by you. Do you have any idea what immediate tasks may be on someone else's list of To Do's? Probably not. Why? Because you have no idea what they feel is truly important to them. The same is true of you. You'll quickly learn that the key to the Passion Path System is not allowing the world to dictate to you what is or is not important.

- **The Highest Short Term Card**– This card keeps your primary goals in focus one at a time.

- **The Highest Long Term Card** – This card keeps your future goals in mind.

- **The Ultimate Dream Card** – This card reminds you of why you're doing all of this in the first place. This is your absolute, biggest dream that would make your life everything you could ever hope it could be.

- **The Most Important Habit Card** – This card keeps you on the path of self-improvement by constantly reminding you of the habits you wish to have in your life and the habits you wish to eliminate. Again, one habit at a time.

- **The Highest Trivial Card** – This card reminds you of the small things that usually get forgotten and allows you to perform small tasks to gain a sense of accomplishment when energy or motivation is low.

- **The Highest Purchase Card** – this card focuses your attention on your most affordable Needs. While you may have the entire list of Wants at the forefront of your mind, the Passion Path System reminds you that your Needs come first. The real fun comes when all of your Needed purchases have been taken care of. You're mind is clear and you can then begin to buy the things you Want.

There are also two other cards we need to find.

- **The Highest Dream Card** – This card gives you an immediate Dream to shoot for this year. You still have your Ultimate Dream Card of course, but this is the Dream you will work to achieve specifically this year.

- **The Easiest Card** – The sole purpose of this card is to always provide a simple task to help you gain momentum when distractions or lack of motivation have prevented you from pursuing your goals.

Remove each of the seven highest priority cards from the seven category piles. The Highest Dream Card may very well be the second card in the Dreams category, but if that Dream cannot be achieved in the next year, move down to the next card until you find the Dream that can be achieved this year. Then remove this Dream Card and keep it with the others.

The Easiest Card is the Trivial task card that is the quickest and easiest to achieve regardless of Priority, Need, or Want. This Card should be dirt simple like "Throw out the garbage" or "Clean off the desk". Whatever the absolute easiest task is within your entire stack of Trivial cards, remove that card and keep it with the others.

You should now have nine cards separated from the others. Keep these nine cards with you at all times. These are your highest priority Destiny Cards. You now have a crystal clear view of what you Need and Want to do. You not only know what needs to be done Immediately, but you also know where your Path – Your Passion Path – will take you. You know your next specific Short Term Goal, Long Term Goal and which Habit to tackle right away. You know where your Passion Path ends up with the culmination of your Ultimate Dream and the achievement of your Highest Dreams along the way. And while you're at it, you know all of the Trivial tasks you need to attend to. And if all else fails, you know the Easiest Trivial task in your entire Destiny Card set just in case you need a little push to get started.

Now that you've determined your Ultimate and Highest Dreams, go ahead and write them on your Ground Zero Page under you Life Purpose.

The process from here is very straight forward. Once you complete a card, save it in a stack of completed cards to admire at the end of the year and grab the next highest priority card in the same category. This way, you're always working on only one task in each category at any given time, giving you focus and permission to stay the course.

There's just one last step. Hang in there! It's pretty easy.

I have learned over time that the nature of an average day's events is structured in such a half-hazard way that it is oftentimes impossible to achieve anything at all. With that in mind, it quickly becomes a painful realization that making plans to achieve just one single task in a day can sometimes be impossible. Crazy as that sounds, we've all been there. We plan out an entire day of tasks and then life just gets in the way. Before you know it you haven't even started and it's lunch time. So you step up and get started and the time flies by. Next thing you know, the sun is setting and you haven't even finished the one task you set out to do. Oh sure, you managed to check your e-mail, get gas, buy groceries, go to work, pick up the kids, pay the phone bill, pick up the dry cleaning, etc. But that one seemingly simple task just didn't get done.

The Passion Path System was designed with this in mind. We don't try to trick ourselves into believing in the ideal system that can get it all done in spite of life. That's just not going to happen. Instead, we plan on life getting in the way and act accordingly.

On your Ground Zero Page, you'll see a section titled "My Calendar Days". Listed below are seven categories and the days of the week with lines beside them. On each line, write the category of task you will work on during that day. Commit yourself to at least one hour that you have set aside just for that task.

Some tasks, like trivial tasks, won't take an hour. In that case, once you finish the first Trivial task, go to the next prioritized Trivial card in the stack and work on it. After an hour, if you can keep working on tasks, continue as long as you can. Other tasks may take much longer than an hour. The idea is to commit yourself to an hour in the hopes that anything you can do for an hour you can do for two or three or the rest of the day. It's a starter task. But if in the end you can only give an hour, then you have achieved at least that much. Pat yourself on the back. After all, if you count all the hours you haven't worked on your goals in the past, it would quickly add up to weeks and months of wasted time. This way, you're actually making progress and motivating yourself on a daily basis. And each day brings different goals and tasks so it doesn't become boring or arduous. If you get burned out on Immediate tasks one day, you can feel relieved to know that the next day you've scheduled to work on Long Term tasks or to focus on your Habits or better yet, go shopping on your Trivial/Purchases day! Eventually, you get into a routine and you start eliminating tasks very quickly because each day brings a fresh perspective on your goals.

You may choose to place any category on any day depending on how well you work on certain days and what your existing schedule requires of you.

For me, Mondays have always been difficult. I don't know why. I don't go out drinking on Sundays. In fact, I usually take it easy on Sundays. But Monday rolls around and I'm just not motivated. Some might call it a case of "The

Mondays" because they don't like their job, but I actually enjoy my job and my schedule is very open regardless of the day. So for whatever reason, I schedule Trivial tasks for Monday. At the very least, if I'm feeling particularly unmotivated, I can achieve the Easiest Trivial Card. Often that's just enough to get me rolling.

For your schedule, consider which tasks might be more compatible for certain days. Would you be more inclined to work on your Dreams on Friday or would you be too distracted by the start of the weekend? If your payday falls on the same day of the week, you might consider scheduling your Trivial tasks on that day and then use the money to knock out some of your Purchases.

The day you assign for Immediate Tasks should be your best day; the day you get things done. For me that's Saturday. I wake up early and start wiping out tasks as quick as possible. Consider your week and assign the remaining categories; Short Term, Long Term, Habit day. On the day you schedule to work on Habits, you can read about how to stop certain habits or better yet, you can spend an entire hour practicing the habit you want to maintain. On your Dream day, plan, design, research, make phone calls, take photos, visit people, check out locations, etc; anything associated with your dream.

Once you've completed the daily task, you should concentrate on your Immediate cards. The Passion Path

System is a daily process. The one hour category days are just a way to keep it interesting and to help you maintain a minimal level of effort. Once you've done the task from the category scheduled for that day, it's important that you continue with your Immediate Tasks. If you run out of Immediate tasks, you move on to the Short Term and Long Term Tasks. Don't worry about running out of tasks though. There are always new tasks cropping up to keep you busy.

And finally, you should always have a day of the week that you allow yourself not to have to achieve anything. Yes, you read that right. It's important to remind yourself once a week that you are justified to take time off because you are actively pursuing your goals and dreams every other day of the week with a detailed system that has made you much more productive than you ever were before. Give yourself permission to slack off just one day. You deserve it.

For me, It's Sunday. Sunday has always been a day when I enjoy doing as little as possible. And I plan ahead to make sure I don't have to do anything if I don't want to. Sometimes my Saturdays are crazy just so I can look forward to doing absolutely nothing the next day. Your body needs a day of rest. But more importantly your mind needs down time without any expectations. Schedule a day of rest and then make sure that everyone around you knows that day is off limits. Let them know that they can have your undivided attention any other day, but that day is yours. It's important.

Your weekly schedule can be in any order, but one day must be left blank as your day of rest, and the remaining days may only have one category assigned to each. Purchases are combined with Trivial Day as one category so you can have a nice day of shopping along with your Trivial tasks.

If you have partnered with someone who also has their own set of Destiny Cards, you can assign at least one hour to any day in addition to the category for that day for what we call Goals Day. This can be particularly useful on your Trivial Day. While you're knocking out relatively simple tasks for yourself, you can be helping someone else with a card they have. For example, if I plan to knock out a few purchases on my Trivial Task day, I may ask my wife if she needs anything while I'm out. You can offer to do more of course. The importance of setting aside this time on the same day is so that those who may need your help know that they can depend on your help at least for an hour on that day. You each have a Goals Day and it's nice to know that on your Goals Day you can ask the other for help with a task without it feeling like an imposition.

Goals Day is one of our favorite days. We both look forward to it on our weekly calendars because it provides time in a specific way to be helpful to someone you love as a sign of respect for their goals and genuine interest in their success. And on the flip side, it's a day when you can expect a little help with tasks that's are just in your way, preventing you from getting other more important things done. It also teaches you how to delegate tasks effectively, which becomes very important in Book 3: Living Your Dreams.

We both have each other's Goals Day on our weekly calendar to remind us. We routinely ask for help on those days with short lists of tasks that we'd love to eliminate. It's not an imposition because we both know ahead of time that we've set aside these days to help each other. Sometimes, one of us will get so caught up in our daily routine that we'll forget it's our Goals Day and it's always a welcome break when the other comes by and asks, "What can I help you with on your Goals Day today?" What a relief. It's also a good feeling to be able to offer help in this way.

The Passion Path System uses several new methods to keep you on track and motivated. You've already seen how the Destiny Cards are used to remind you of the things you need to do. But knowing what to do and being motivated to do them are two different things. How many times have you created a To Do list only to look at it and think "I don't want to do any of this stuff." The Passion Path System makes it a lot easier by forcing you to look at just one task at a time. And to make that even easier, each category of task is assigned a different day of the week according to your schedule. So on any given day of the week, you know you only have to be concerned with one task. And if you finish that task, the next card is waiting right behind it.

Don't feel like you're locked into just the cards you've already written either. You can add new cards to any category at any time. Just make sure you prioritize them properly by Need or Want and Importance.

It's a good idea to take some time at the end of the day to clear your mind. By this time, it's too late for you to do much of anything else and it's very therapeutic to keep your head clear, particularly before going to sleep. At this time, keep a stack of fresh index cards and a marker handy and jot down everything that might be bouncing around in your head; things to do, people to call, errands, repairs, whatever. Get it out of your head. The next day, prioritize these new cards with the rest of your Destiny Cards and live happy in the knowledge that you'll get to them when they need to be done in the proper order.

Each New Year, I like to come up with a word or phrase that best describes how I plan to tackle the coming year. I write the year and this word or phrase on a card and leave plenty of room below to write little hash marks for each card I achieve throughout the year.

The hash marks are for counting each card you complete, no matter what category it was in, except habits – you never really eliminate Habits. Keep Habit cards in sight to remind you of the habits you wish to maintain or eliminate. Time has proven that it takes no less than two weeks to form a habit, but it can take a lifetime to eliminate one.

For each completed card, you draw a simple hash mark. After the forth hash mark, you draw the fifth hash mark by crossing the other four diagonally. Each diagonally crossed group counts for five completed tasks.

This is my Yearly Theme Card. At the end of the year, I wrap up all of my completed cards with a big rubber band and put my Yearly Theme Card right on top. I count up all of the hash marks and write the total number of achieved cards in big numbers right on top.

Although my wife and I maintain our own separate Destiny Cards, we like to combine the completed cards to see what we've achieved together. Our first Yearly Theme Card was titled "New Beginnings". We were trying the Passion Path System and Destiny Cards for the first time and we had high hopes of achieving quite a bit. We did. The next year's them was "Living Deliberately". We learned a lot of lessons that first year and were now on top of our game and making deliberate choices in our lives; some of which were a bit painful. The next year's theme was "Passions". We had our lives under control and were actively pursuing our Greatest Passions with a level of energy and focus we had never before imagined possible.

When we first started using The Passion Path System in our lives, we achieved 16 cards. The next year, it was 29 cards. The year after that, 36 cards. And then things really started to heat up. We started to notice a cumulative effect building upon itself. We had systematically eliminated so many nagging Immediate and Short Term tasks that we found ourselves actively pursuing bigger and more courageous goals and passions. We were also able to work on Long Term Goals that required daily effort toward the completion of huge projects; things like converting old music cassettes to mp3's for our music collection, backing up huge amounts of data on all of our computers, consolidating, scanning and organizing photos.

The yearly number of completed tasks just grew and grew. Your stack of completed cards will grow larger and larger just as ours did. It got so amazingly effective and rapid that the nerd in me decided to write a second book on how to implement the Passion Path System using the latest software and technology. I had to, the next year we completed 460 cards! By February of the following year we had already achieved 283 cards in just two months! It was fantastic and I love to look at the stacks of cards from each successive year as a reminder of just how amazing The Passion Path System and Destiny Cards are. But the techno-geek in me knew there were others like me who would have cards in the thousands and technology was the best way to go for those rocketeers.

It is comforting to know however, that no matter how many tasks and goals and passions you can come up with, the Passion Path System can handle it with just a stack of index cards and a marker.

Believe it or not, you've already completed one card. Grab an index card and write the sentence, *"Discover My Life Purpose and Greatest Passions"*. If you went through the exercise and discovered your Life Purpose and Greatest Passions, this task is achieved. Mark a hash on your Yearly Theme Card and place the completed card behind the Theme Card to start a stack of all the cards you complete this year. At the end of the year you can read all of the completed tasks you have achieved and you can keep the stack of completed cards out to remind you of your success.

The Passion Path System can be fun and a real team builder for the family. For example, when making purchases, choose a high dollar item to save for. For every small dollar item you buy, put aside 10% of the purchase price into a savings account to save for that large dollar item. This supports progress toward high dollar items while eliminating guilt one little piece at a time.

On a daily basis, review all of your Highest category cards. Read your Life Purpose, Greatest Passions, and Dreams on your Ground Zero Page often to remind you of what's important to you. Play a game with yourself to see how quickly you can eliminate cards. If you live with someone, consider displaying your highest category cards so they can know what's important to you and possibly help you achieve them. It's better if every member of the family has their own set of cards. Often you'll find that your cards coincide with their goals in one way or another and your combined efforts can make things progress even quicker. In fact, it's important that you do not try to force one set of cards to work for more than one person. This can lead to choices and decisions based on guilt or compromise and that is against everything this system is about. After all, no two people can have exactly the same Life Purpose and Greatest Passions.

By eliminating your Needs before your Wants, you put your life in order so you can enjoy your Life Purpose and Greatest Passions. As I mentioned, using this system has a cumulative effect. As you progressively eliminate items from your cards, you begin to accumulate more time and resources to get things done. Each completed card, no matter how trivial, is a step toward achieving your Dreams. Remember, "A goal not written down is just a good idea."

Eventually, you find your Needs have been met and you're now devoted to achieving your Wants. And living your Life

Purpose and Greatest Passions without hindrance or debilitating needs is the very definition of a well lived life.

Review and brainstorm your Destiny Cards on a regular basis; at least every six months, preferably every three. But don't get caught in the details. This system is here for you, not the other way around. There are no deadlines unless you accept them. There is no guilt for inaction. If you achieve something notable that's not on a card, make one and put it with the other completed cards and put a hash mark on your Yearly Theme card for a task well done. The calendar days are a guide for when you don't know what to do next. If you're working on something that interests you, then stay with it – regardless of the calendar day. The whole idea is to keep yourself motivated and moving toward your Dreams.

In the next couple of chapters we talk about the enemies; Procrastination and Fear. So far, we've shown you how to discover your true purpose in life and the things that you feel passionate about. We've given you all the tools to get organized and prioritized. And we've even shown you how to help someone else with their goals and expect the same in return. But if we don't show you how to overcome procrastination and fear, you could be stopped in your tracks.

So read on, because in the next chapter we show you that procrastination isn't real and in Chapter 6, you'll find out that neither is fear!

A problem well stated is

a problem half solved.

- Charles Kettering

Inventor – Holder of 140 patents
President of General Motors 1920-1947

Chapter 5
Procrastination

On the next page is a graphical depiction of the eleven level medieval maze found at Chartres Cathedral near Paris, France. It's actually more of a winding path than a maze. Just for fun, trace the path from the bottom to the center with a pencil. You'll quickly notice a repeating theme where you get so close to the center that you think it's much easier than you originally imagined. But then you realize that you keep following similar paths and getting nowhere – sometimes closer, sometimes far away. The Chartres maze is a brilliant metaphor for life.

THE MEDIEVAL CHARTRES MAZE

The Chartres Maze has been around since the twelfth century. There are tens of thousands of full-sized versions of the Chartres Maze around the world. They're usually located near universities, churches or other religious sites. There are nearly 2,000 in the U.S. and over 200 in California alone. My favorite is the one located inside Grace Cathedral in San Francisco.

The purpose of these mazes is to simply walk along the path and pray, meditate or reflect upon personal challenges. As I mentioned, the path is a metaphor for life. The center represents our goals and dreams. Each path is a lesson in life; some short and easy, others long and difficult. We normally perceive paths leading toward the center as "good luck" and paths leading away as "bad luck." These are definitions based on random thinking. With Life Purpose in mind, there is no random thinking. Paths leading away from the center are distractions. Paths that pass each other are our habits of trying to do the same things over and over again expecting different results. Turning points near each other are the same distraction at different times and points of view in our life.

My wife and I were walking this very maze one weekend at the Grace Cathedral when the bells tolled the hour. The reverberating sound of those bells, surrounded by towering walls of granite and stained glass was breathtaking. All the more impressive as we were both walking this metaphor for life. It was an incredibly profound experience.

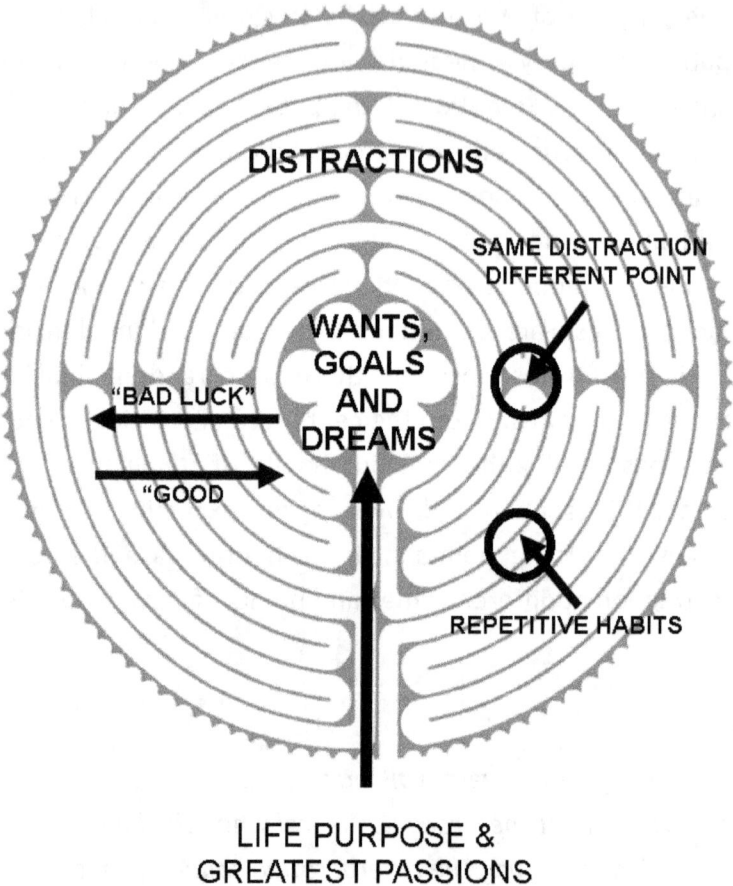

DISTRACTIONS

SAME DISTRACTION
DIFFERENT POINT

WANTS,
GOALS
AND
DREAMS

"BAD LUCK"

"GOOD"

REPETITIVE HABITS

LIFE PURPOSE &
GREATEST PASSIONS

By thinking in a non-random manner, we now perceive paths leading toward the center as Purpose-driven decisions. The problem with distractions is that they allow procrastination and fear to enter into our lives. Distractions can vary from mild to catastrophic; anything from losing our keys to a death in the family. With each distraction, you are faced with one of three choices;

Action, Inaction or Indecision. Remember the Sierpinski Triangle.

But how do you make non-random decisions? Simple, by learning your Life Purpose. When you know your Life Purpose, you automatically filter every decision you make through that Purpose. By definition, this makes all of your decisions non-random. By living your Life Purpose, you begin to achieve cumulative results that inevitably lead to the attainment of your ultimate dreams.

Now let's get something cleared up right away. There is no such thing as "Procrastination". Procrastination is nothing more than a label which describes a host of symptoms. The word "lazy" is just as worthless. It has become far too easy to just hang a label on the simple problem of getting started on something you need to do and chalk it all up to human failure. That is such rubbish. Nobody is lazy. And no one procrastinates. We are either passionately motivated to do something or we're not. It's as simple as that. And that passion can be direct or indirect. Which is a good thing because if the only way to get truly excited about something is to have a direct passion for it, some tasks would never get done.

Ask any kid to rake the leaves in the yard and there's a good chance they may appear lazy or procrastinating. But tell the same kid that the only way they can go to their friend's house to play is if the leaves are raked up, you'll see some instant, indirect passion for leaves. Suddenly all of the procrastination and "laziness" is gone.

What we know as procrastination is really just one of three conditions. The good news is that they can all be remedied very easily. The first condition is in the form of physical challenges such as pain, illness, fatigue, stress or chemical depression. These symptoms represent a bigger problem; a condition of physical health that should be addressed. Over-the-counter pain relievers can give you a quick fix, but it is important to investigate these issues with a doctor. It could be something as simple as being overweight, needing to supplement your diet with vitamins, more exercise, or in extreme cases, a chemical imbalance requiring medication.

The second condition is one of mental perspective. This is manifest in feelings of boredom, guilt, fear, or event-based depression such as loss of a job or a loved one. Just as with the physical health issues, these mental health issues can hold you back. But the treatment is much different. While depression is a very real and debilitating condition, if it is event-based rather than chemical, it is a matter of perspective, which can be corrected. The same is true of guilt and fear. And boredom is simply a lack of imagination. Ask any young kid (that isn't staring at a video game screen these days) what they do for fun outside and I'm positive you'll have a long list of very imaginative ideas. All of these conditions exist because of the manner in which you see the world. A person with strong religious convictions compared to an atheist will have very different viewpoints on guilt. We'll talk more later about fear, but it too is nothing more than perspective which can be adjusted.

The third condition is a result of external distractions such as lack of organization, overwhelming workload, lack of resources, more enjoyable diversions and noise. These too are easily resolved. Being organized is just a matter of taking the time to "sharpen your axe". And if you don't know how, there are plenty of resources to teach you how. If your workload is overwhelming, you merely need to ask for help while learning to say the most powerful word in the world, "No!" A lack of resources is a very common problem. However, necessity truly is the mother of invention. And if you really need to achieve something but don't have the resources to do it, you can get creative and find a solution. We have enjoyable diversions all over the place; television, radio, video games, friends, the beach. To conquer these in the twenty-first century can be a very daunting task. But it is possible with a little planning and self-control. And finally, noise is just a matter of headphones or ear plugs.

As you may have guessed by now there are no excuses for not getting things done. But this still does not address the desire to get things done that you're not all that passionate about. Being motivated to do the things you're directly passionate about is easy. And you can even indirectly blackmail yourself to get things done that you are not passionate about so you can reward yourself with the things you are. Sure, if I asked you to do something associated with your personal Life Purpose, you would have no trouble whatsoever. It comes natural to you. But chores and errands can feel like anchors to your progress, weighing down your life. That is until you realize that once you know your Life Purpose, the chores and errands that remain in your life are all directed to making your Life Purpose shine. It's an automatic process too. With your Life Purpose solidly entrenched in your mind, you automatically judge each and every choice that comes your way according to how well it fits your Life Purpose. The rest just fall away along the wayside. They're no longer a part of your life. And you don't feel any guilt for doing so either because you know your true calling and to behave contrary to your Life Purpose is simply unhealthy.

Still, we find ourselves "procrastinating" and being "lazy". Sometimes even when it's about something we feel very passionate about. Why? Because we haven't taken the time to figure out why. This happens all of the time because we don't know where to start. We don't know what questions to ask. Well, now we do.

The wonderful news is there are several techniques to help you overcome procrastination. In the Workbook, starting on page 145, there are Reference Pages that review the information below so you'll have it handy whenever you need it. Whenever you find yourself facing a task that you just don't have any passion for, the first thing you should do is ask yourself if it is truly compatible with your Life Purpose. If it isn't, then the solution is simple; dump it on someone else or toss it altogether. If it is compatible but you're still having trouble finding your motivation, these techniques will help you get back on track.

Trap and Tag – Usually the biggest problem of motivation is simply trying to figure out why you're not motivated in the first place. Take the time to think about the task. Imagine doing it and then pinpoint what's holding you back. Is it a physical challenge such as pain, fatigue or stress? Is it a mental challenge such as boredom, guilt or fear? Or are you just too distracted in your current environment? Do you need to get away? Do you feel like you don't have enough information to get started? Once you figure out what's holding you back, you've successfully trapped and tagged the "animal". You can then act to resolve the issue with better information.

I often find myself stuck and unmotivated simply because I don't have enough information to get started. And it's not until I take the time to figure this out that I can then begin to formulate the right questions to the right resources. I have successfully trapped and tagged my "animal"; an external distraction based on the simple fact that I am lacking resources in the form of useful information.

For example, the power steering in our car had a huge leak. I looked under the hood, but I'm a computer guy; I don't know what I'm looking at in there. I can see there's a lot of gunk all over the place and there is acrid smoke coming off of the engine. I know this is not a good thing, but now what? I bought a service manual, but for some odd reason it doesn't even show where the power steering pump and hoses are located. How can I repair it if I don't know where it is or what it looks like? Is it the hose? Is it the pump? The seals? I have no idea. A serious lack of information. I don't think I can repair it myself. I don't even own a car jack or stands. And my lack of information doesn't stop there. I eventually give in and decide to take it to an auto mechanic. Which one? Do I look in the phone book? The Internet? Ask a friend? Can I trust the mechanic once I decide on one? How much is it going to cost? How long will it take to get my car back? Do I need to rent a car in the meantime? I think I'll just relax on the couch and watch TV.

I know that my Life Purpose gets me into just enough trouble to stick my nose into a situation like this because I am explorative by nature. What IS under the hood of this thing? What does a power steering pump look like anyway? How does it work? Why is mine leaking all over the place? But I also know that my Life Purpose has nothing to do with being mechanically inclined so I can automatically and guiltlessly delegate the situation to someone else; the mechanic.

But if I did have a Life Purpose that was more mechanically inclined, I would know right away that I had what it takes to get this situation resolved – as long as I had taken the time to trap and tag to figure out that my lack of motivation was caused by a simple lack of information.

Do Nothing – This is a lot harder to do than you might think. I don't mean to just ignore the issue. I mean force yourself to do absolutely nothing for five minutes. It's not as easy as it sounds! No music. No TV. No reading. No discussion. Nothing! Just sit there. And don't fall asleep! Two things will begin to happen pretty quickly; you'll realize that doing nothing is really, really boring and your mind will begin to come up with all kinds of better things to do. Take that energy and creativity and focus it on the problem at hand. And don't do anything until you have an answer – or at least a pretty good idea of how to start. If you don't know where to begin, consider the next technique.

Slice and Dice – Just about any task can be broken down into smaller, more manageable steps. Break up the problem into as many small chronological steps as possible. Then attack them one at a time. One of the biggest mistakes I would commonly make would be to put a task on my To Do List like "Finish writing book". That's a really loaded task. Anything that needs to be "finished" was once started and never completed, which means there is a lot to it. Just putting a task on my list saying "finish it" was not clear enough and often lead to complete inaction. I learned to break up tasks like this into steps such as "Write the table of contents", "Write the Introduction". And "Write Chapter 1".

This technique can be repeated several times until you literally end up with a list of tiny steps. Of course you don't want to get too ridiculous, but as long as each step is a valid step in the right direction, who's to say what is too tiny of a step?

Laugh at the Fear – We'll talk much more about fear later in chapter six. Suffice it say for the moment that fear is a controllable emotion. And not by some life-long meditation technique or a nihilist realization of your own imminent death. No, fear can actually be transmuted into healthy excitement by doing nothing more complicated than simply laughing while finding a cause to be excited about. Seriously, this is something I have found incredibly helpful in my own life. We'll discuss the science and practice of this technique a little later. It's pretty cool actually.

Talk smack – When you tell somebody you're going to do something, you're more apt to do it. Call it guilt, honor, whatever, you put yourself in plain view of people who now have expectations of you. So, let everybody know what you plan to do, and when. Trust me, they will hold you to it. This works particularly well for tasks that scare the mess out of you. You feel the fear, but you force yourself to do it anyway because you're friends and family are watching.

Dive In – This is the best way to overcome procrastination. Do something; anything in connection with the task at hand. It takes mere minutes to simply put something away, but hours of self-nagging if you procrastinate cleaning up. Commit yourself to just five minutes on the task and plan a break after that. Chances are you'll continue working and forget all about the break. Simply stand up (knowing a break is in your future). Just getting onto your feet or walking toward something is enough to break the bonds of procrastination. I do this all the time. I know I should be doing something other than sitting around, so I stand up and wait until I figure out what it is.

Another approach is to identify the most difficult task or part of a task and tackle it first. If you knock the "ugly" out of a task right away, then the rest of the clean-up is easy. My favorite motto is "Do it Now! Do it Ugly! Make it pretty later…"

Talk it out – Try writing out your feelings about the thing you are postponing in a journal. Ask yourself why you have failed to do what you know should be done. Tell yourself what you're going to do and when. Try using a recorder and record what you say to yourself so you can play it back later. If you're so inclined, meditate or pray about your concerns. If talking to yourself doesn't get you moving, try talking it out with another person. Sometimes, just putting the situation into words for someone else to understand can spark the desire to get moving.

Pros & Cons – Benjamin Franklin's favorite technique was to make a list with two columns. On the left column, he would list all the reasons for procrastinating. On the right he would list the benefits of doing the task in question. He would then compare the two sides. Whichever side looked best was the deciding factor.

I have used this technique countless times. And it is amazing when you take the time to do this just how clear the whole situation quickly becomes. And it can go either way. I've had lists show me that the task really wasn't all that important in the first place. More often than not though the list showed me I was being a big baby.

Quick Cures – There are also quick cures for emotional "procrastination" or lack of motivation. For each emotion, there is a quick solution. Again, these are listed on your Reference Pages in the back of the book.

- When you feel fear, just dive in. You won't die. Trust me.

- When you feel pain or fatigue, plan ahead for later.

- When you feel sad, watch a comedy or a stand-up act.

- When you feel depressed, listen to uplifting music.

- When you feel inferior, dress up and look in the mirror.

- When you feel uncertain, speak up about what you DO know.

- When you feel poor, imagine your dreams coming true.

- When you feel incompetent, remember your past achievements. Review your completed Destiny Cards!

- When you feel insignificant, remember your goals.

With a firm handle on procrastination, you will more easily be able to live your Life Purpose and Passions and achieve your Dreams by constantly deciding to act. Now let's take a hard look at that other fallacy; fear.

Most people would rather be certain they're miserable than risk being happy.

- **Robert Anthony**

Psychotherapist and personal performance trainer

Chapter 6

Fear

Fear is the greatest challenge we all face in living our Life Purpose and Greatest Passions. But happily, it's all a trick of the mind.

Zig Ziglar (a famous self-help guru) created the acronym "F.E.A.R."; False Evidence Appearing Real. In any situation, your brain is designed to offer your mind options to consider - fear is just one of many. However, the human brain has a protective negative design bias. It is programmed to offer poor choices for effective action in an effort to protect you from harm. There are over eighty (80) defined emotions, two-thirds of which prevent action.

And there are over 450 documented phobias! ALL of which prevent action. And action is key to living your Life Purpose. Your Life Purpose, Passions and Dreams are pointless if you're frozen by fear. And it doesn't help that what you've been taught about fear is wrong.

Biological fight or flight is not a 50/50 choice. There are actually 3 choices; Action, Inaction and Indecision. Remember the Sierpinski Triangle? The brain is designed for fight, flight or freeze. And only one of these choices results in effective action. Again, your mind is biologically programmed to do nothing two out of three times! The brain's protective negative design bias is in full force. We've also been told that the opposite of fear is courage. That's not true either. Courage is action in spite of fear. The opposite of fear is knowledge.

Here's a story to illustrate my point. Consider a library engulfed in flames. The librarian is trapped in the building. She's terrified. She has no idea which direction to run or what to do. Questions flood her mind as she looks in every direction at once to find a safe exit or haven within the building. She's faced with the same three decisions we all face; fight, flight, or freeze. Does she try to fight the fire? Does she run and jump out of a window? Or does she tremble in fear in one spot while she tries to figure out what to do?

Suddenly, a fireman runs into the library. He's not terrified at all. In fact, he's excited. But the conditions for both he and the librarian are exactly the same. They're both in a burning building. The difference is the fireman has knowledge that transmutes his perception of the same situation into excitement rather than fear. How is that possible?

The librarian is untrained in fire fighting and has little if any experience in dealing with the inside of a burning building. She's afraid of every true and imagined aspect of the situation. But the fireman has been well trained in dealing with all kinds of fires and conditions. He knows that while the fire and smoke are very dangerous if not handled properly, the greater danger is actually hidden in the basement where the floor the librarian is standing on is supported by trusses.

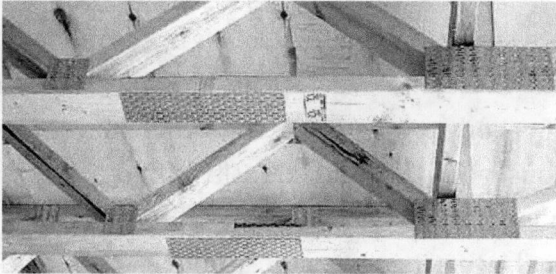

Trusses are an excellent, light weight, means of construction that save money and time and work very reliably as a support structure – when they're not on fire. Firemen hate trusses. They are built with far fewer materials in an angular pattern to support just as much weight as a much heavier and more expensive wooden plank. So they're more of a financial advantage than a structural one because they require fewer materials to manufacture and weigh much less to transport. But when trusses catch on fire, they burn faster than wooden planks and become unstable very quickly. The fireman knows this and is in a heightened excited state, ever observant of the tell-tale signs on the floor that might show points of weakness or failure that could cause him and the librarian to plunge into the fiery basement. The librarian however is terrified of everything. Yet she doesn't even know the real dangers she's facing with the one thing she figures she might be able to rely on the most; the floor. Remember, the opposite of fear is not courage, it's knowledge. Keep this in mind as I describe the varying levels of emotional intensity that are involved in this story. We'll come back to the poor librarian in a second.

There are seven documented levels of emotional Intensity. All seven share the exact same physiological symptoms; breathing, body temperature and general level of agitation or nervousness. Only the intensity differs. That is curious enough in itself, but it gets better. With each increase in emotional intensity, your perception changes quickly from a positive, enjoyable sensation to a negative one and stays negative through subsequent levels as your emotional intensity increases. If it weren't for level six, the magic level, we would only know the positive emotion of love followed by six increasing levels of horror. And it's that magic sixth level that gives us the power to control our fears. But I'm getting ahead of myself.

The first and least intense emotional level is sympathy and love. This is a positive emotion. Your breathing is easy, body temperature is comfortably warm and your nerves are calm.

The second level is disgust and hate. This is the first of a long line of negative emotions. Your breathing is shallower. Your body temperature begins to rise. And your nerves start to get on edge.

The third emotional level is anger and rage. Your breathing is much faster. Your body temperature approaches the boiling point and your nerves are so wound up that your stomach is rigid and tight.

The forth level is sadness and despair. Obviously a negative sensation, but an odd turn occurs with your physiology. Your breathing actually becomes labored and restricted. Your body becomes cold, but your stomach is in a knot.

The fifth level of emotional intensity includes worry, fear, paranoia and terror. Your breathing is practically halted. Your body temperature is not only cold but your skin may also become clammy. And your stomach fells sickly and hard as a rock.

But then, all of a sudden, at level six a strange thing occurs. The intensity of level six is greater than any of the other five we've discuss so far. But it's a positive emotion, even more powerful than love. At level six, we experience feelings of happiness, excitement and even elation. The body warms up again. Breathing is fast and furious. But your nerves are off the chart! Your stomach is like granite, it even hurts, but you don't care. You feel great! Just think of the times you've ridden a roller coaster or gone snow tubing or water skiing. And isn't it funny how, for no reason at all, you start to laugh? Where did this incredibly intense and positive emotion come from after all of the negativity of the last four levels of intensity?

It's no accident. It's part of our built-in fight, flight or freeze genetic encoding and it's exactly at this level so that you can be at your absolute best when faced with the final seventh level. Here lies the key to overcoming your fears. Level seven is horror and revulsion. Your body is at its limit to cope at this point. You're not breathing at all. Your body is literally frozen in its tracks. The blood in your extremities is rushing to the core of your body. You even begin to lose the color in your face. And your nervous system is so confused the best you can achieve is to freeze in your tracks.

In the story about the fireman and the librarian, the fireman knows the real dangers. He's concerned, but he chooses to be excited in order to act effectively. Running into burning buildings excites him – in spite of the dangers, which he knows in great detail. "Choice" is the operative word here. By simply choosing to allow the intensity of the situation to increase from level five (fear) to level 6 (excitement), the fireman effectively transmutes his emotional state. This is a counter-intuitive behavior. Most people will tell you to "calm down", when what you really need to do is get excited! The old saying goes, "Fear is all in your mind." Actually, fear is all in your brain. Fear is just one of many options your brain offers your mind. It's up to your mind to properly perceive a given situation and choose the correct option. In this case, the fireman has simply chosen to intensify the physiological symptoms of fear into excitement. But how exactly? How can the librarian do the same without the benefit of the specialized training the fireman has? By finding a cause; a crusade.

The second the librarian realizes a cause for action, her mind will be distracted from the paralyzing fear and she'll instantly transmute her fear into excitement. That cause could be anything from seeing children trapped in the library or a particularly rare collection of books in danger of being destroyed. The moment she decides to act, her mind is dedicated to resolving the cause. All of the negative choices the brain was offering up earlier are replaced with excited options to get the situation resolved. The librarian becomes just as excited as the firemen in the same situation but for different reasons. You can do the exact same thing with your fears.

The probability of something undesirable happening and the fear of it happening are two completely different things. But neither are actually real! Fearing a probability is an exercise in mental torture. You're just beating yourself up over nothing. The only way we learn is to succeed or fail. And both require action. Procrastination due to fear merely prolongs the inevitable outcome you need! Success or failure is irrelevant. You need to learn the lesson.

Let me tell you another story. This one is a true story about Thomas Edison. Tom had been working on the light bulb for years. He meticulously tested every material he could think of. In the end, after over two hundred attempts with materials that didn't work, he settled on the unlikely solution of carbon–infused bamboo. But that was after crazy ideas like tightly spun cotton, brass tubes and even the skin off the top of pudding! Seriously! When he had finally made the electric light bulb a viable solution, he was interviewed by a newspaper reporter who asked him how he felt about wasting his time on over two hundred failed attempts to make the light bulb. Thomas Edison replied that each attempt was not a failure. They were all equally valuable lessons in how NOT to build a light bulb.

The brain has an amazing imagination. It can conjure up hundreds of ways to fail. And there is only one perfect way to succeed. The probability of achieving the perfect solution is impossible. Your results will always be somewhere in between. So make the worst of it! Remember my motto, "Do it Now! "Do it ugly! Make it pretty later..." Getting anything past the initial creation stage will put you far ahead of the game. From there, it's just a matter of improving. It's always easier to improve something than to try to create perfection from the start.

The number one killer of fear is action. Doing what you fear eliminates it. And surprisingly, you can trick your brain into thinking you have conquered the fear by simply pretending. Not just visualizing, but actually physically acting out what you fear. The sensory signals your brain receives from your muscles in concert with your imagination are exactly the same data your brain records when you actually perform the act you fear. Continual practice will lessen the severity of the fear to a point where you can more easily act upon it in reality.

You've probably seen examples of this in movies when people act as if they're giving a speech or practicing what they might say in a meeting. The simple act of going through the motions is enough for the brain to register effective action. So the next time the brain is faced with the actual event, it's not a shock, it's been "here" before. An even more amazing example is the use of this technique in therapy for persons with severe phobias of heights or spiders. The patients are fitted with video goggles that completely cover their field of vision and then gradually exposed to virtual simulations of the things they fear. Studies have shown astonishing improvement using this technique.

So let's take a look at your fears. On page 143, list all of your fears and phobias in no particular order in the column on the left. As before, try to fill every line. Fear of heights, enclosed places, spiders, rejection, failure, success, illness, loneliness, you name it.

In the column on the right, sort the list in the left column from least to greatest intensity. You may be surprised how difficult this sorting can be. Are you more afraid of spiders than heights? More afraid of enclosed places than spiders? It may help to compare just the first two fears on the list and decide which you are afraid of the least and then repeat the process with the next word until you go through the entire list.

Once you have sorted your fears from least to greatest intensity, go to your Ground Zero Page, and write your top three least intense fears in the Courage Plan section on page 152.

Your Courage Plan from this point is very simple. Every day, choose the least intense fear listed in the Courage Plan section of your Ground Zero Page. Use the techniques we discussed in this chapter to progressively eliminate the least intense fear on your list one at a time. These techniques are also included in the Reference Pages in the Workbook.

Imagine the fear. Dismiss the fear as one of many options your brain has served up for you to consider. Embrace and increase the intensity of the fear to a level of excitement by finding a cause to be excited. Let that excitement become something to laugh about – just like on the roller coaster. This is your life! Physically act out the thing you fear while you imagine success. Be the fireman! Know your fear. Get excited. Then actually do the thing you fear.

And congratulations! You just created your Courage Plan. Go ahead and create a new Destiny Card with the sentence "Create My Courage Plan" and hash it as complete with your yearly Theme Card. You're well on your way to defeating your fears and living your Life Purpose and Greatest Passions.

One machine can do the work of fifty ordinary men.
No machine can do the work of one extraordinary man.

- Elbert Hubbard

American writer, publisher, artist, and philosopher

Chapter 7
Your Unique Abilities

If you have not yet eliminated a fear, you can still use it to your advantage. Unique Abilities show you how to use your Assets in concert with your Challenges to create synergistic tools that are tailor-made for your specific needs.

Your Assets are the qualities, talents and skills that make you who you are; artistic, mathematically inclined, organized, sociable, physically fit, etc.

Your Challenges are the conditions and attitudes that prevent you from acting. This includes the 3 categories of procrastination and the fears you listed in your Courage Plan.

> **Synergy:** *The working together of two things to produce an effect greater than the sum of their individual effects.*
>
> **Compromise:** *An accommodation in which both sides make concessions and neither get what was originally required.*
>
> *Synergy is far more functional than compromise. But we're taught compromise because it's much easier and quicker to come to a decision somewhere in the middle than to take the time and effort necessary to create a truly unique and mutually beneficial synergistic solution.*

Synergistic Tools are combinations of both your Assets and your Challenges to form Your Unique Abilities. We're told we should try to ignore or minimize our weaknesses. But our weaknesses are actually our strengths because they create pathways and approaches that work specifically for us in ways that don't work for anyone else.

On page 144 in the Workbook, on the left, under Assets, list your qualities, talents and skills. You may look back at page 136 under Positive Qualities in Your Life Purpose to help jog your memory. Don't worry about the grouping lines or numbers - that comes later. List as many items as you can come up with. You don't have to fill every line but it's best if you can.

On the right, under Challenges, list the things that keep you from doing the things you need and want to do in life. These include the things you most often procrastinate about and all of your fears you listed on page 143. So go ahead and copy your fears over from that page. And then add the things you usually procrastinate about. Again, try to fill every line.

Consider the physical, mental and external challenges you face. You can always add to these lists later.

So now let's play a game. I call it the Power Tools Game. The rules for the Power Tools Game are simple.

1. Find a single die with six sides.
2. Roll the die.
3. Take one Asset matching the number you rolled on the die from the first Assets group and circle the number.
4. Roll the die again.
5. Take one Challenge matching the number rolled with that number from the first Challenges group.
6. Combine the two words and write them in the Unique Abilities section on your Ground Zero Page.

Repeat this process a couple of times. Use the next group of Assets and Challenges for each turn. If you roll a number and the line for that number is blank, use the last word in that group.

Don't worry if they don't make sense right away. There is a trick that puts them into clear perspective. Can you guess what that trick is? I'll give you a hint; they were created using a random process which we have already proven gives ordinary results. And what piece of information transforms random into non-random to produce extra-ordinary results? That's right, Life Purpose. When you combine randomly generated Unique Abilities with your Life Purpose, a Power Tool emerges. These Power Tools always have a meaning special to you because they are derived from your unique Qualities, Behaviors, Assets and Challenges. And they all have value. But it's up to you to interpret their importance for yourself. Some power tools may seem very simplistic. Others may be immensely profound. But, they can only make sense to you. When they make sense, it will become obvious what you can do with them. But they may not make sense right away. Sometimes you have to let your subconscious mind work them over for a while.

Let me tell you a story the stand-up comedian Lewis Black once shared during his show. He mentioned that he was in a restaurant and overheard the phrase, "If it weren't for my horse, I wouldn't have spent that year in college." This is a very strange thing to say even in context. But this was the only part of the conversation he heard and it made no sense to him at all. In fact, he joked that it caused him no end of frustration because to him it seemed unfathomable for the circumstances described to occur at all, let alone for anyone to ever think to say something like that. But the comment was presumably quite rational to the person who said it. The moral of this story is, her comment made perfect sense to her, but it made no sense whatsoever to him. And that's okay. The same thing is true of your Power Tools. If you come up with a Power Tool of "Creative Sand Sharks" and it makes sense to you, then so be it. That's what makes it a Unique Ability that only you can use.

The Power Tools Game is an exercise to get you started on thinking creatively about yourself. It's about widening your perception to include new possibilities and interpretations of your Unique Abilities.

So how do you use these Unique Abilities? The idea is to take Challenges and turn them into advantages by using your Assets with them, not against them. It's not about working through your Challenges. It's about embracing your Challenges as unique parameters for your Assets to work with. And it's not about using your Assets to circumvent your Challenges either. The idea is to use both your Assets and your Challenges to create completely new behaviors. These are your specific, Unique Abilities. No one else has them. You'll use them to your advantage to accomplish your goals like super powers that only you possess. When you know these things about yourself, you become a much more capable person. And an added bonus is the more you use your challenges, particularly your fears, the less debilitating they become.

Here are some examples:

Example #1:

Asset: Artistic
Challenge: Shy
Life Purpose: Innovative Thinker
Unique Ability:

> *The Innovative Thinker can use her art to express herself and her far reaching ideas to initiate social interaction without words to a level that makes people come to her to continue the "conversation" she started – her way.*

Example #2:

Asset: Computer savvy
Challenge: Short
Life Purpose: Compassionate Listener
Unique Ability:

> *The short Compassionate Listener can fit in a cubicle more easily with another person who needs their help with a computer problem. And their compassion helps them know when to stop explaining and let them learn the lesson on their own.*

Example #3:

Asset: Patient
Challenge: Soft voice
Life Purpose: Witty Teacher
Unique Ability:

> *The Witty Teacher can teach his students more effectively by getting them used to listening for soft-spoken, witty, subtle jokes he sneaks into the lesson instead of trying to yell over his students to be heard.*

Example #4:
(an example of one of my own Unique Abilities)

Asset: Excellent at mathematics
Challenge: Fear of heights
Life Purpose: Explorative Archivist
Unique Ability:

> *When I decide to go on vacation to the Grand Canyon, I can do the math and realize that since the canyon is a little over a mile deep, and it takes fifteen seconds to achieve terminal velocity, if I fell in and scrunched up to do a cannon ball in the river, I would hit the water at about 200 mph. Compensating for the depth, temperature, speed and salinity of the water, I would still fire out the other side of the planet somewhere in India. Laughing at that helps me to transmute my fear and get me excited to see the Grand Canyon. After all, I've never been to India.*

This is a game. So have fun with it! You can also combine multiple Assets and Challenges to create even more powerful Tools. Combine three related challenges with two assets or vice-versa. This is who you are. So make the best of it.

While you're at it, go ahead and create a Destiny Habit card with the sentence "Play the Power Tools Game" on it and prioritize it with the rest of your Habit Destiny Cards.

You have now created a starter set of synergistic power tools. And you have scheduled time to form a habit of creating more for yourself in the future.

Your Ground Zero Page is now complete! Rip it out of the back of the book along with the Reference Pages and keep them on you at all times along with your nine highest Destiny Cards. Refer to them often - At least once a day.

Now sit back and relax! Realize just how powerful you have become in just a short time. You know your Life Purpose. You know your Greatest Passions which excite you to truly live your life every day. You know how to eliminate procrastination and fear from your life. And you have specially designed power tools that work only for you based on your Unique Abilities to affect powerful decisions and actions in your life. Your Ultimate Dreams are now well within your grasp. You just have to choose to act!

If you're not going to be yourself, who else are you going to be?!

\- Scott A. Rossell

**Life Purpose: Explorative Archivist
Author, researcher, explorer**

Chapter 8

Get Ready To Live!

Forming the habit of making non-random decisions is simply a matter of remembering to do so. It helps to have printed reminders or talismans that constantly serve to prompt your mind into action on your Life Purpose and Greatest Passions. The most important reminder of course is your Ground Zero Page. You can also use famous quotations, pictures that show what your dreams might look like or a piece of jewelry like a necklace, ring or bracelet that has significant meaning to you.

I even have a personal totem; a symbol of an animal that best fits my personality and reminds me to stay true to the calling of my Life Purpose.

My totem is the Laughing Falcon. The Laughing Falcon is a very specific bird. It primarily hunts snakes. And after it catches a snake it lets out a call that sounds like a big chuckle of a laugh. Sometimes it even finishes with a fast little giggle. This symbol has special meaning to me because I enjoy exposing the "snakes" in the world in the form of wrong thinking, old ideas, or just plain lies and thrashing them to "death" for all to see as I laugh and giggle at their demise.

My father's totem was a Grey Wolf. Anyone who knew him would understand the connection right away. He was a strong man with an astonishingly keen eye for observation and human behavior with salt and pepper hair and a confident walk.

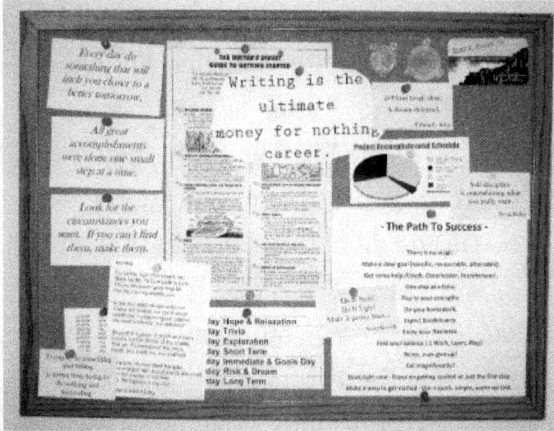

The point is to find things that keep you moving toward your goals; your Highest and Ultimate Dreams, your Greatest Passions on a daily basis. I have a bulletin board in my office that is covered with all kinds of quotes and lists and poetry to remind me every day of what is important to me. There's even a seven sided English coin stuck up there. And it doesn't matter if anyone else understands what these things are. They only need to be important to you to remind you of what you truly want from your life.

It's strange that we would have to constantly remind ourselves of something so apparently obvious once we know our Life Purpose and Greatest Passions, but it's true. We're constantly bombarded by television, radio, taxes, car repairs, laundry, politics at the office, rude people, family obligations, soccer practice, Saint Patrick's Day, you name it. It's easy to forget where you were headed with your dreams when every day brings you problems to solve and chores to sort out. Just imagine how tough it would be if you DIDN'T know your Life Purpose and Greatest Passions! If you DIDN'T know your Unique Abilities and how to overcome procrastination and fear. If you DIDN'T...You DID do all of the exercises in the book right?

You're already well on your way to a nice stack of completed Destiny Cards representing accomplished goals for the year. You should have at least three cards completed already. You've discovered your Life Purpose and Greatest Passions. You've created your Courage Plan. And You've discovered some very specialized, synergistic Power Tools by examining your Unique Abilities.

I'd like to thank you for the opportunity to share my insights on a subject that I am very passionate about. I look forward to hearing from you and sharing the excitement of your successes on our website. And I'm not just saying that. With my Life Purpose as an "Explorative Archivist", I love and live to explore and to record my findings. I explore new restaurants, books, movies, music, that street I've never turned down, that building I'm having an interview in...and the success and joy of people I have touched with my ideas. It is at the core of my being. Just like your Life Purpose is to you.

Once you know your Life Purpose, you can never think or act randomly again. Your life is on auto-pilot with the proper direction and guidance every second of every day zooming toward your dreams. And it's a great feeling!

This book has given you everything you need to
Get Ready To Live!

So get out there and...

Start Living!

- Recommended Reading -

100 Simple Secrets of Successful People
David Niven, Ph.D., 2006
ISBN: 0-06-115793-7

All You Can Do is All You Can Do
but all you can do is enough!
A.L. Williams, 1988
ISBN: 0-8041-0499-9

The Art of Living
The Classic Manual on Virtue, Happiness, and Effectiveness
Sharon Lebell, 1995
ISBN: 0-06-251346-X

Discover What Your Best At
Barry and Linda Gale, 1982
ISBN: 0-671-69589-4

Do It! Let's Get Off Our Buts
John-Roger and Peter McWilliams, 1991
ISBN: 0-93-158079-X

Doing It Now
Edwin C. Bliss, 1984
ISBN: 0-553-27875-4

Don't Sweat the Small Stuff at Work
Richard Carlson, Ph.D., 1998
ISBN: 0-7868-8336-7

Don't Sweat the Small Stuff with Your Family

Richard Carlson, Ph.D., 1998
ISBN: 0-7868-8337-5

Do What You Love, The Money Will Follow

Marsha Sinetar, 1989
ISBN: 978-0440501602

Easier Than You Think

Richard Carlson, Ph.D., 2005
ISBN: 0-06-075888-0

Feel the Fear and Do It Anyway

Susan Jeffers, Ph.D., 1987
ISBN: 0-449-90292-7

First Things First

Stephen R. Covey, A. Roger Merrill and Rebecca R. Merrill, 1994
ISBN: 0-684-80203-1

Goal-Free Living, How to Have the Live You Want Now!

Stephen M. Shapiro, 2006
ISBN: 978-0-471-77280-4

How to Win Friends & Influence People

Dale Carnegie, 1936
ISBN: 978-0-671-72365-1

Instant Gold

Frank O'Rourke, 1964
ISBN: 978-1594263019

Jonathan Livingston Seagul, a story

Richer Bach, 1970
ISBN: 0-380-01286-3

My Life Has No Purpose
David Weber, 2009
ISBN: 978-0-557-19654-8

The Passion Test
The Effortless Path to Discovering Your Destiny
Janet Attwood and Christ Attwood, 2006
ISBN: 1-59540-835-5

The Richest Man in Babylon
George S. Clason, 1955
ISBN: 0-525-48441-8

The Secret
Rhonda Byrne, 2006
ISBN: 1-58270-170-9

Simplify Your Life
100 Ways to Slow Down and Enjoy the Things That Really Matter
Elaine St. James, 1994
ISBN: 0-7868-8000-7

StrengthsFinder 2.0
Tom Rath, 2007
ISBN: 978-1-59562-015-6

Think and Grow Rich
Napolean Hill, 1937
ISBN: 0-449-91146-2

Type Talk
Otto Kroeger and Janet M. Thuesen, 1988
ISBN: 0-385-29648-7

Understanding Yourself

Phoebus Publishing Company, 1977
ISBN: 0-415-13453-2

Working With Difficult People

Muriel Solomon, 1990
ISBN: 0-13-957390-9

And just for fun...

The Ultimate Hitchhiker's Guide to the Galaxy

Douglas Adams, 2002
ISBN: 0-345-45374-3

World War Z

Max Brooks, 2006
ISBN: 978-0-307-34661-2

The House on the Strand

Daphne du Maurier, 1969
ISBN: 978-0812217261

- Notes -

- Notes -

- Notes -

- Notes -

Study Workbook

<u>My Life Purpose</u>

Positive Qualities

Organized, sociable, observant,
compassionate, strong, etc…

Behaviors & Activities

I am happiest when I am
doing / being / having…

_____	_____
_____	_____
_____	_____
_____	_____

<u>My Life Purpose</u>

Sort and Combine Behaviors & Activities

Catch-All Section

<u>My Greatest Passions</u>

#1 Greatest Passion (Life Purpose):

_____

Milestones:

1. _____
   _____
   _____
   _____
   _____
   _____
   _____

2. _____
   _____
   _____
   _____
   _____
   _____
   _____

3. _____
   _____
   _____
   _____
   _____
   _____

<u>My Greatest Passions</u>

#2 Greatest Passion:

_____

Milestones:

1. _____
_____
_____
_____
_____
_____
_____

2. _____
_____
_____
_____
_____
_____
_____

3. _____
_____
_____
_____
_____
_____

<u>My Greatest Passions</u>

#3 Greatest Passion:

_____

Milestones:

1. _____
   _____
   _____
   _____
   _____
   _____
   _____

2. _____
   _____
   _____
   _____
   _____
   _____
   _____

3. _____
   _____
   _____
   _____
   _____
   _____
   _____

<u>My Greatest Passions</u>

#4 Greatest Passion:

_____

Milestones:

1. _____
_____
_____
_____

2. _____
_____
_____
_____

3. _____
_____
_____
_____

My Greatest Passions

#5 Greatest Passion:

_____

Milestones:

1. _____
_____
_____
_____
_____
_____
_____

2. _____
_____
_____
_____
_____
_____
_____

3. _____
_____
_____
_____
_____
_____
_____

<u>My Courage Plan</u>

Fears & Phobias	Sorted from Least to Greatest Intensity
_____	1. _____
_____	2. _____
_____	3. _____
_____	4. _____
_____	5. _____
_____	6. _____
_____	7. _____
_____	8. _____
_____	9. _____
_____	10. _____
_____	11. _____
_____	12. _____
_____	13. _____
_____	14. _____
_____	15. _____
_____	16. _____
_____	17. _____
_____	18. _____
_____	19. _____
_____	20. _____
_____	21. _____
_____	22. _____
_____	23. _____
_____	24. _____
_____	25. _____

<u>My Unique Abilities</u>

Assets	**Challenges**
Qualities, Talents & Skills	Physical, Mental & External Forces and Fears

1. _____
2. _____
3. _____
4. _____
5. _____
6. _____

1. _____
2. _____
3. _____
4. _____
5. _____
6. _____

---

1. _____
2. _____
3. _____
4. _____
5. _____
6. _____

1. _____
2. _____
3. _____
4. _____
5. _____
6. _____

---

1. _____
2. _____
3. _____
4. _____
5. _____
6. _____

1. _____
2. _____
3. _____
4. _____
5. _____
6. _____

---

1. _____
2. _____
3. _____
4. _____
5. _____
6. _____

1. _____
2. _____
3. _____
4. _____
5. _____
6. _____

<u>Reference Pages</u>

The Passion Path System

1. Get a stack of index cards and a large felt tip marker.
2. Find a large flat surface on which to write and sort cards.
3. Brainstorm to get everything out of your head onto the cards.

   > Think about the office, the house, garage, vehicles, friends, relatives, hobbies, repairs, purchases, vacations, things learn, habits to eliminate and all your dreams, big and small.

4. Write a sorting header card for each category and sort your cards into seven stacks:
   - Immediate
   - Short Term
   - Long Term
   - Dreams
   - Habits
   - Trivial
   - Purchases
5. Sort from most important to least.
6. Sort Purchases from lowest to highest cost.
7. Write Need or Want in the top right corner of each card.
8. Move the Needs cards to the top.
9. Write the category and year on the top of each card.
10. Take the first card from each category as your highest priority card.
11. Find the Easiest Trivial card.
12. Find the Highest Dream that can be achieved within a year.
13. Create your yearly theme card with the year and theme name and room to make hash marks for completed cards.

You should now have nine total cards which represent the highest priorities in every category, your easiest task to get you started, your Ultimate Dream and your Highest Dream for the year.

Daily Destiny Card Routine

1. Your daily schedule has at least one hour dedicated to work on a task in the assigned category for that day of the week.

   For example, Monday's are my Trivial Tasks Day because me and Monday's just don't get along.

2. If you have a partner using the Destiny Card System, one of the days of the week should have at least one hour scheduled to help them on their Goals Day and vice-versa.

3. Work on your Highest Immediate card every day.

4. When you complete an Immediate card, move on to your next Highest Immediate card until you run out of Immediate cards.

5. When you run out of Immediate cards, move on to your Highest Short Term Card.

6. If you find yourself left with only Long Term Cards, it's time to review your cards and brainstorm again.

The Sierpinski Triangle

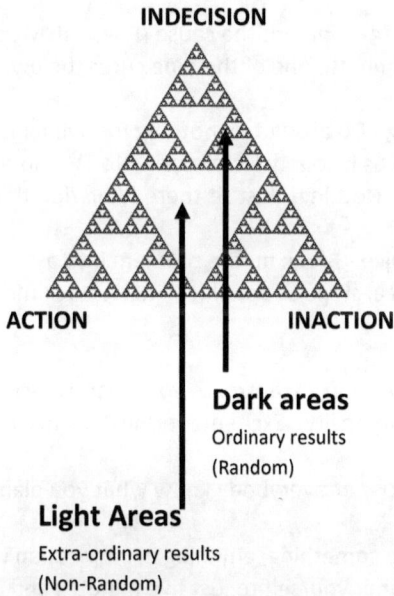

INDECISION

ACTION INACTION

Dark areas
Ordinary results
(Random)

Light Areas
Extra-ordinary results
(Non-Random)

Dreams are always Extra-Ordinary.

Three Categories of Procrastination

- **Physical Challenges**
  Pain, illness, fatigue, stress or chemical depression.

- **Mental Challenges**
  Boredom, guilt, fear, or event based depression such as
  loss of a job or loved one.

- **External Distractions**
  Lack of organization, overwhelming workload, lack of
  resources, more enjoyable diversions or noise.

Eight Anti-Procrastination Techniques

- **Trap and Tag** - Pinpoint the cause (Physical, Mental or External) then use one of the nine cures (below).

- **Do Nothing** - Do absolutely nothing for five minutes. It's not as easy as it sounds! No music. No TV. No reading. No discussion. Nothing! Just sit there. And don't fall asleep!

- **Slice and Dice** - Break up the problem into as many small chronological steps as possible. Then attack them one at a time.

- **Laugh at the Fear** - Transmute your fear by increasing emotional intensity. Excitement is just a smile away.

- **Talk smack** - Let everybody know what you plan to do.

- **Dive In** - Do something; anything in connection with the issue. Commit yourself to just five minutes and plan a break afterwards. Chances are you'll continue working and forget all about the break. Simply stand up. Just getting onto your feet or walking toward something is enough to break the bonds of procrastination. Identify the most difficult task or part of a task and knock it out first thing.

- **Talk it out** - Write out your feelings about the thing you are postponing in a journal. Ask yourself why you have failed to do what you know should be done. Tell yourself what you're going to do and when. Record what you say to yourself so you can play it back later. Meditate or pray about your concerns. Then act on your first impressions.

- **Pros & Cons (Benjamin Franklin's favorite)** - List your reasons for procrastinating. List the benefits of doing the task in question. Compare the two lists. Which one looks better?

Nine Cures for Procrastination

- When you feel fear, just dive in. You won't die. Trust me.

- When you feel pain or fatigue, plan ahead for later.

- When you feel sad, watch a comedy or a stand-up act.

- When you feel depressed, listen to uplifting music.

- When you feel inferior, dress up and look in the mirror.

- When you feel uncertain, speak up about what you DO know.

- When you feel poor, imagine your dreams coming true.

- When you feel incompetent, remember your past achievements. Review your completed Destiny Cards!

- When you feel insignificant, remember your goals.

Eliminate Your Fears

Knowledge

- F.E.A.R.: False Evidence Appearing Real (Zig Ziglar)
- Fear is an option, not a requirement.
- Your brain is designed to offer your mind options to consider.
- Your brain has a protective negative design bias programmed to offer poor choices for effective action.
- Of the 80+ emotions 2/3rds are negative.
- There are 450+ documented phobias.
- The opposite of fear is knowledge, not courage.
- Courage is acting in spite of fear.
- Knowledge is knowing there is nothing to fear.

Realization

- There are 7 emotional intensity levels.
- All 7 levels have the same physiological symptoms.
- Fear is of a <u>lesser</u> intensity than excitement.

Take Action or Pretend To

- Transmute fear into excitement by simply smiling and laughing.
- Find the excitement in a cause.
- If you can't act, pretend to. Both in your mind and in physical action.
- Doing what you fear, even faking it, reduces and eventually eliminates the fear.

Ground Zero Page

Life Path Anniversary Date: _____

My Ultimate Dream:

_____

My Highest Dream:

_____

My Life Purpose: I am a(n)...

_____   _____

#1 Greatest Passion (Life Purpose):   **#2 Greatest Passion:**

_____   _____

Milestones: Milestones:

1. _____   1. _____

2. _____   2. _____

3. _____   3. _____

#3 Greatest Passion: **#4 Greatest Passion:**

_____   _____

Milestones: Milestones:

1. _____   1. _____

2. _____   2. _____

3. _____   3. _____

#5 Greatest Passion:

_____

Milestones:

1. _____

2. _____

3. _____

My Calendar Days:

Assign one category to each day of the week.
Dedicate at least one hour each day to that category.
If you have a goals partner, let them know which day is your Goals Day.

Immediate Day	-	Eliminate those nagging tasks.
Short Term Day	-	Keep your goals in focus.
Long Term Day	-	Keep your future goals in mind.
Dreams Day	-	Plan in detail until you can do.
Habit Day	-	Create the good and eliminate the bad.
Trivial/Purchases Day	-	Remember the small things.
Day of Rest	-	Total relaxation! Clear your mind.
(Goals Day)	-	At least one hour for a loved one.

Monday _____

Tuesday _____

Wednesday _____

Thursday _____

Friday _____

Saturday _____

Sunday _____

My Courage Plan:

Your top three sorted list of fears in order of intensity, lowest first.

1. _____

2. _____

3. _____

My Unique Abilities – Power Tools:

1. _____ _____

2. _____ _____

3. _____ _____

www.ingramcontent.com/pod-product-compliance
Lightning Source LLC
LaVergne TN
LVHW021456080426
835509LV00018B/2299